175 Yummy Peanut Butter Cookie Recipes

(175 Yummy Peanut Butter Cookie Recipes - Volume 1)

Erma Ketron

Content

175 Awesome Peanut Butter Cookies Recipes

***

1. 3 Ingredient Peanut Butter Cookies

Serving: 24 | Prep: 10mins | Ready in:

Ingredients

- 1 cup peanut butter
- 1 cup white sugar
- 1 egg

Direction

- Preheat an oven to 175°C/350°F>
- Use electric mixer to mix egg, sugar and peanut butter till creamy and smooth in bowl; roll mixture to small balls. Put on baking sheet; use fork to flatten each, creating crisscross pattern.
- In preheated oven, bake for 10 minutes; cool cookies for 2 minutes on baking sheet. Put on plate.

Nutrition Information

- Calories: 98 calories;
- Total Fat: 5.6
- Sodium: 52
- Total Carbohydrate: 10.5
- Cholesterol: 8
- Protein: 3

2. 5 Ingredient Peanut Butter Chocolate Cookies

Serving: 16 | Prep: 10mins | Ready in:

Ingredients

- 1 cup creamy peanut butter
- 1 egg
- 1/4 cup stevia sweetener (such as Truvia®)
- 2 tablespoons unsweetened cocoa powder
- 1 tablespoon vanilla extract

Direction

- Set an oven to preheat to 175°C (350°F).
- In a food processor or a mixer, mix together the vanilla extract, cocoa powder, stevia sweetener, egg and peanut butter. Roll the dough into one-inch balls. On an ungreased baking tray, put 1-2 inches apart. Use a fork to flatten the balls.
- Let it bake in the preheated oven for about 10 minutes until the edges are set. Allow it to cool for 10 minutes on the baking sheet.
- Use waxed paper to line a tray. Place the cookies onto a tray for about 15 minutes until they cool down to room temperature; let chill in the fridge for 30 minutes.

Nutrition Information

- Calories: 105 calories;
- Total Carbohydrate: 5.8
- Cholesterol: 12
- Protein: 4.6
- Total Fat: 8.5
- Sodium: 79

3. Almond Y Peanut Butter Oatmeal Cookies

Serving: 48 | Prep: 15mins | Ready in:

Ingredients

- 1 3/4 cups all-purpose flour
- 2 teaspoons baking soda
- 1/2 teaspoon salt
- 1 1/4 cups peanut butter
- 1 cup butter, cut into small chunks
- 3/4 cup white sugar
- 3/4 cup packed brown sugar
- 2 eggs
- 1 teaspoon vanilla extract
- 1/2 teaspoon almond extract (optional)
- 1 1/2 cups quick-cooking oats

Direction

- Preheat an oven to 175°C/350°F>
- Sift salt, baking soda and flour in bowl.
- Use electric mixer to beat brown sugar, white sugar, butter and peanut butter till creamy and smooth in bowl. One by one, beat eggs into creamed butter; beat well prior to adding next egg. Mix almond extract and vanilla extract in.
- Mix flour mixture slowly into creamed butter mixture till incorporated fully; use wooden spoon to fold oats in. Roll dough to 1-in. balls; put on baking sheet, 1-in. apart. If desired, press fork into every cookie.
- In preheated oven, bake for 12-15 minutes till cookies are lightly browned.

Nutrition Information

- Calories: 128 calories;
- Protein: 2.8
- Total Fat: 7.6
- Sodium: 139
- Total Carbohydrate: 13
- Cholesterol: 18

4. Apple Peanut Butter Oatmeal Cookies

Serving: 24 | Prep: 20mins | Ready in:

Ingredients

- 3 eggs
- 2 cups cinnamon applesauce
- 1 cup peanut butter
- 1/2 cup brown sugar
- 2 teaspoons vanilla extract
- 3 cups rolled oats
- 1 cup all-purpose flour
- 1 cup flax seed meal
- 1/2 cup whole wheat flour
- 1 1/2 teaspoons baking soda
- 1 1/2 teaspoons ground cinnamon
- 2 apples - peeled, cored, and cut into small cubes

Direction

- Preheat oven to 175 degrees C (350 degrees F).
- In a bowl, whip vanilla extract, brown sugar, peanut butter, applesauce and eggs together till becoming smooth.
- In a separate bowl, mix cinnamon, baking soda, whole wheat flour, flax seed meal, all-purpose flour and oats together. Mix egg mixture into the oat mixture and put in apples; whisk till equally blended.
- Roll dough into golf ball-sized balls and put 2 inches apart on the baking sheets.
- Bake for roughly 12 minutes in the preheated oven till cookies become golden.

Nutrition Information

- Calories: 204 calories;
- Total Fat: 8.8
- Sodium: 142
- Total Carbohydrate: 26.5
- Cholesterol: 23
- Protein: 6.6

5. Basic Peanut Butter Cookies

Serving: 18 | Prep: 15mins | Ready in:

Ingredients

- 1/4 cup butter
- 2 cups Basic Cookie Mix
- 1/2 cup peanut butter
- 1 egg
- 1 teaspoon vanilla extract

Direction

- Preheat an oven to 180°C/350°F.
- Melt butter on low heat; mix into Basic Cookie Mix. Mix lightly beaten egg and peanut butter in. Add vanilla; stir well.
- Form to 1-in. balls with lightly floured hands; put on greased cookie sheet, 2-in. apart. Bake till golden for 12-15 minutes. Cool for a few minutes. Transfer from cookie sheet to racks; finish cooling.

Nutrition Information

- Calories: 69 calories;
- Sodium: 55
- Total Carbohydrate: 1.5
- Cholesterol: 17
- Protein: 2.2
- Total Fat: 6.4

6. Best Peanut Butter Cookies Ever

Serving: 36 | Prep: 30mins | Ready in:

Ingredients

- 2 cups peanut butter
- 2 cups white sugar
- 2 eggs

- 2 teaspoons baking soda
- 1 pinch salt
- 1 teaspoon vanilla extract

Direction

- Set the oven to 175°C or 350°F to preheat and coat cookie sheets with grease.
- In a medium bowl, stir together sugar and peanut butter until smooth, then beat in one egg at a time. Stir in vanilla, salt and baking soda, then roll the dough into balls with 1 inch size. Arrange balls on the prepped cookie sheet with 2 inches apart. Use the back of a fork to press into the top with a criss-cross.
- In the preheated oven, bake about 8-10 minutes. Let cookies cool on baking sheet about 5 minutes prior to transferring to a wire rack to cool thoroughly.

Nutrition Information

- Calories: 132 calories;
- Total Fat: 7.5
- Sodium: 140
- Total Carbohydrate: 13.9
- Cholesterol: 10
- Protein: 3.9

7. Better Butter Cookies

Serving: 48 | Prep: | Ready in:

Ingredients

- 2 1/4 cups all-purpose flour
- 1 tablespoon baking soda
- 1 cup butter
- 3/4 cup white sugar
- 3/4 cup packed brown sugar
- 1/4 cup peanut butter
- 3 eggs
- 3 tablespoons vanilla extract
- 1/2 cup chopped walnuts (optional)

Direction

- Preheat an oven to 175°C/350°F.
- Sift baking soda and flour; put aside. Cream brown sugar, butter and white sugar in medium bowl; one by one, beat eggs in then peanut butter and vanilla. Add dry ingredients to creamed mixture; mix till combined. Mix nuts in.
- By heaping teaspoonfuls, drop on cookie sheets; in preheated oven, bake for 12-15 minutes. On wire racks, cool.

Nutrition Information

- Calories: 103 calories;
- Cholesterol: 22
- Protein: 1.6
- Total Fat: 5.7
- Sodium: 112
- Total Carbohydrate: 11.5

8. Cake Mix Cookies VI

Serving: 36 | Prep: 10mins | Ready in:

Ingredients

- 2 eggs
- 1/3 cup water
- 1/4 cup margarine
- 1 cup peanut butter
- 1 (18.25 ounce) package yellow cake mix
- 2 cups semisweet chocolate chips

Direction

- Preheat an oven to 175°C/350°F then grease cookie sheets.
- Cream peanut butter, margarine, water and eggs in big bowl; blend cake mix in well. Fold chocolate chips in; by rounded spoonfuls, drop on prepped cookie sheet.

- In preheated oven, bake for 8-10 minutes; cool cookies for 5 minutes on baking sheet. Transfer to wire rack; completely cool.

Nutrition Information

- Calories: 164 calories;
- Total Fat: 9.6
- Sodium: 149
- Total Carbohydrate: 18.5
- Cholesterol: 11
- Protein: 3.2

9. Caramel Nougat Bar Peanut Butter Cookies

Serving: 18 | Prep: | Ready in:

Ingredients

- 1/2 cup white sugar
- 1/2 cup packed brown sugar
- 1/2 cup butter
- 1 teaspoon vanilla extract
- 1/2 cup peanut butter
- 1 egg
- 1 1/2 cups all-purpose flour
- 1/2 teaspoon baking soda
- 1/2 teaspoon baking powder
- 1/4 teaspoon salt
- 36 fun size bars milk chocolate covered caramel and nougat candy

Direction

- Cream the egg, peanut butter, vanilla, butter or margarine, brown sugar and white sugar.
- Put in salt, baking powder, baking soda, and flour.
- Wrap 1 heaping tsp. of dough around a bite sized milk chocolate covered caramel and nougat candy bar. Bake for 13 to 16 minutes at 175°C or 350°F. Allow it to cool down for 5 minutes prior to taking out of the pan.

Nutrition Information

- Calories: 337 calories;
- Sodium: 216
- Total Carbohydrate: 46.4
- Cholesterol: 27
- Protein: 4.7
- Total Fat: 15.3

10. Chef John's Peanut Butter Cookies

Serving: 12 | Prep: 5mins | Ready in:

Ingredients

- 1/2 cup unsalted butter
- 1/2 cup white sugar
- 1/2 cup packed brown sugar
- 1/2 cup creamy peanut butter
- 1/2 teaspoon kosher salt
- 1/2 teaspoon baking powder
- 1/2 teaspoon baking soda
- 1 egg
- 1 1/4 cups all-purpose flour

Direction

- In a stand mixer, whip baking soda, baking powder, salt, peanut butter, brown sugar, white sugar and butter till becoming smooth.
- Scrape down the sides of the bowl and beater using a spatula. Put in egg and stir for roughly 60 seconds.
- Stir in flour gradually using the mixer on low setting. Scrape down the sides of the bowl and beater. Mix on medium setting for roughly half a minute till combined.
- Shape dough into a ball, use plastic to cover and let chill in the refrigerator for 2 to 3 hours.
- Preheat the oven to 190 degrees C (375 degrees F).

- Portion out cookie dough in equal-sized balls on the baking sheet covered with a silicone baking mat. Roll dough into smooth balls by moistened hands. Stamp each ball using a fork with a crisscross pattern.
- Bake in the preheated oven till becoming golden, about 10 minutes.
- Let stand on the baking sheet for 5 minutes prior to removing to the cooling rack.

Nutrition Information

- Calories: 252 calories;
- Total Fat: 13.6
- Sodium: 229
- Total Carbohydrate: 29.5
- Cholesterol: 36
- Protein: 4.7

11. Chewy Chocolate Peanut Butter Chip Cookies

Serving: 60 | Prep: 15mins | Ready in:

Ingredients

- 1 1/2 cups butter, melted
- 2 cups white sugar
- 2 eggs
- 1 teaspoon vanilla extract
- 2 cups all-purpose flour
- 3/4 cup unsweetened cocoa powder
- 1 teaspoon baking soda
- 1/2 teaspoon salt
- 2 cups peanut butter chips

Direction

- Preheat an oven to 175°C/350°F.
- Mix sugar and butter in big bowl; beat vanilla and eggs in. Mix salt, baking soda, cocoa and flour; mix into butter mixture slowly. Mix peanut butter chips in; by rounded teaspoons, drop on ungreased cookie sheets.

- In preheated oven, bake for 8-10 minutes. Cool for 1 minute. Transfer to wire racks; completely cool.

Nutrition Information

- Calories: 132 calories;
- Cholesterol: 18
- Protein: 2.6
- Total Fat: 7.2
- Sodium: 96
- Total Carbohydrate: 14.4

12. Chewy Hollow Chocolate Peanut Butter Cookies

Serving: 20 | Prep: 15mins | Ready in:

Ingredients

- 1 1/2 cups white sugar
- 1 1/2 cups brown sugar
- 1/2 cup butter, softened
- 1 cup creamy peanut butter
- 2 eggs
- 1 teaspoon vanilla extract
- 2 cups all-purpose flour
- 1 teaspoon baking soda
- 1 (8 ounce) package chocolate chips

Direction

- Preheat an oven to 175°C/350°F.
- Use electric mixer to beat brown sugar and white sugar till fluffy and smooth in big bowl; beat peanut butter in till smooth. Beat vanilla extract and eggs into sugar mixture till creamy; mix baking soda and flour into sugar mixture till dough is just mixed. Fold chocolate chips in; shape dough to ping pong ball-sized balls. Put on baking sheet.
- In preheated oven, bake for 20 minutes till golden brown. Cool cookies for 10 minutes on baking sheet.

Nutrition Information

- Calories: 323 calories;
- Cholesterol: 31
- Protein: 5.7
- Total Fat: 15.1
- Sodium: 166
- Total Carbohydrate: 44.9

13. Chewy Peanut Butter Chocolate Chip Cookies

Serving: 24 | Prep: 15mins | Ready in:

Ingredients

- 1/2 cup butter, softened
- 1/2 cup peanut butter
- 1 cup packed brown sugar
- 1/2 cup white sugar
- 2 eggs
- 2 tablespoons light corn syrup
- 2 tablespoons water
- 2 teaspoons vanilla extract
- 2 1/2 cups all-purpose flour
- 1 teaspoon baking soda
- 1/2 teaspoon salt
- 2 cups chopped semisweet chocolate

Direction

- Preheat oven to 190 degrees C (375 degrees F).
- Cream white sugar, brown sugar, peanut butter and butter in a big bowl till becoming smooth in texture. Whip in the eggs one at a time, then mix in vanilla, water, and corn syrup. Mix salt, baking soda and flour together; mix into the peanut butter mixture. Fold in chocolate chunks. Drop by 1/4 cupfuls 3 in. apart into the ungreased baking sheets.
- Bake in the preheated oven till edges become golden, about 12 - 14 minutes. Let cookies cool down for 60 seconds on the cookie sheet prior

to transferring to the wire racks to let it cool down totally.

Nutrition Information

- Calories: 246 calories;
- Total Fat: 11.6
- Sodium: 163
- Total Carbohydrate: 33.5
- Cholesterol: 26
- Protein: 4.3

14. Chewy Peanut Butter Cookies

Serving: 18 | Prep: | Ready in:

Ingredients

- 1 cup packed brown sugar
- 1 cup white sugar
- 1 cup peanut butter
- 1 cup shortening
- 1 teaspoon baking soda
- 2 tablespoons hot water
- 2 1/2 cups all-purpose flour
- 2 eggs

Direction

- Mix shortening, peanut butter and sugars. Put baking soda into hot water; add to mixture. Mix well.
- Mix eggs in; add flour then roll dough to balls.
- On ungreased cookie sheets, put balls. Use fork dipped in water to press to create crisscross design. Bake for 8-10 minutes at 175-190°C/350-375°F.

Nutrition Information

- Calories: 346 calories;
- Total Carbohydrate: 39.2
- Cholesterol: 21
- Protein: 6.1

- Total Fat: 19.3
- Sodium: 147

15. Chewy Whole Wheat Peanut Butter Brownies

Serving: 16 | Prep: 20mins | Ready in:

Ingredients

- 1/3 cup margarine, softened
- 2/3 cup white sugar
- 1/2 cup packed brown sugar
- 2 eggs
- 1 cup peanut butter
- 1/2 teaspoon vanilla extract
- 2 tablespoons water
- 3/4 cup whole wheat flour
- 1/4 cup all-purpose flour
- 1/4 teaspoon salt
- 1 teaspoon baking powder
- 1/4 teaspoon baking soda

Direction

- Preheat an oven to 175°C/350°F then grease 9x9-in. baking.
- Beat sugars and margarine in big mixing bowl. One by one, add eggs; beat till mixture is fluffy and light. Mix water, vanilla and peanut butter in.
- Mix baking soda, baking powder, salt and flours in another mixing bowl; mix into peanut butter mixture. Blend well then spread batter in prepped pan.
- In preheated oven, bake for 30-35 minutes till touching top makes it spring back. Cool; cut to 16 squares.

Nutrition Information

- Calories: 222 calories;
- Sodium: 215
- Total Carbohydrate: 24

- Cholesterol: 23
- Protein: 5.9
- Total Fat: 12.6

16. Choco Peanut Butter Cookies

Serving: 36 | Prep: | Ready in:

Ingredients

- 1 1/2 cups packed brown sugar
- 1 cup peanut butter
- 3/4 cup butter
- 1/3 cup water
- 1 egg
- 1 teaspoon vanilla extract
- 3 cups rolled oats
- 1 1/2 cups all-purpose flour
- 1/2 teaspoon baking soda
- 1 1/2 cups semi-sweet chocolate chips
- 4 teaspoons shortening
- 1/3 cup chopped peanuts

Direction

- Preheat the oven to 350°F (180°C).
- Beat margarine, peanut butter and brown sugar until the mixture is fluffy.
- Blend in vanilla, egg and water.
- Add combined baking soda, flour and oats; mix properly. Chill, with cover for 1 hour.
- Form into 1 inch balls. Arrange on ungreased cookie sheet. Press each ball into 1/4-inch thick circles using a sugar-coated glass bottom.
- Bake until edges turn golden brown, for 8 to 10 minutes. Transfer to wire racks, completely cool.
- For frosting: In a saucepan, melt chocolate over low heat. Stir in vegetable shortening, mix until smooth.
- Place 1/2 teaspoon melted chocolate on top of every cookie. Sprinkle chopped peanuts on top, refrigerate until set. Store in an airtight container.

Nutrition Information

- Calories: 205 calories;
- Total Fat: 11.3
- Sodium: 83
- Total Carbohydrate: 23.8
- Cholesterol: 15
- Protein: 4.3

17. Chocolate Coated Peanut Butter Crackers

Serving: 20 | Prep: | Ready in:

Ingredients

- 3/4 cup peanut butter
- 2 pounds vanilla flavored confectioners' coating
- 80 buttery round crackers
- 2 1/4 ounces colored candy sprinkles

Direction

- Spread about 1 tsp. of peanut butter on each of crackers half. Add leftover crackers on top to make peanut butter "sandwiches".
- In the top of a double boiler over hot but not boiling water, melt the vanilla candy coating or chocolate-flavored almond bark. Lower the heat and keep chocolate in top of double boiler above simmering water.
- Dip each cracker "sandwich" into chocolate; let the surplus to drain off back to the pot.
- To cool down, add coated crackers on the wax paper. Drizzle with multi-colored sprinkles or any holiday garnish. Let coating set down totally, adds into the fridge for 15 minutes, if needed. Keep between layers of wax paper in cool and dry spot, or store in the refrigerator. These freeze well, too.

Nutrition Information

- Calories: 389 calories;

- Total Fat: 24
- Sodium: 214
- Total Carbohydrate: 39.3
- Cholesterol: 10
- Protein: 6

18. Chocolate Peanut Butter Bars II

Serving: 12 | Prep: | Ready in:

Ingredients

- 1/2 cup butter
- 1/2 cup packed brown sugar
- 1 teaspoon vanilla extract
- 2 cups peanut butter
- 2 1/2 cups confectioners' sugar
- 2 cups semisweet chocolate chips

Direction

- On low heat, melt the margarine and butter. Put in vanilla, peanut butter and sugars. Stir them well.
- Press into one 9 x 13 in. pan.
- Melt chocolate chips and spread on the top. Allow it to cool down.

Nutrition Information

- Calories: 588 calories;
- Total Fat: 37.8
- Sodium: 258
- Total Carbohydrate: 60
- Cholesterol: 20
- Protein: 12.1

19. Chocolate Peanut Butter Blossom Cookies

Serving: 54 | Prep: 30mins | Ready in:

Ingredients

- Reynolds® Parchment Paper
- 1/2 cup shortening
- 1/2 cup peanut butter
- 1 cup packed brown sugar
- 1 teaspoon baking powder
- 1/8 teaspoon baking soda
- 1 egg
- 1 tablespoon milk
- 1 teaspoon vanilla
- 1 1/2 cups all-purpose flour
- 1/4 cup unsweetened cocoa powder
- 1/4 cup granulated sugar
- Dark chocolate "kiss" candies

Direction

- Preheat oven to 350°F. Line Reynolds(R) Parchment Paper on 2 cookie sheets.
- Beat the peanut butter and shortening in a big bowl using an electric mixer on medium to high speed for half a minute. Put in baking soda, baking powder and brown sugar. Whip till combined, scraping the sides of the bowl once in a while. Whip in vanilla, milk and egg till combined. Whip in as much of the cocoa powder and flour as possible using the mixer, with a wooden spoon at the end if needed.
- Add the granulated sugar to a small-sized bowl. Form the dough into 1-inch balls. Roll the balls in sugar to coat. Put the balls 2 inches apart onto the prepped cookie sheets.
- Bake till edges become firm, about 10 - 12 minutes. Instantly push down a dark chocolate candy into each cookie's middle. Slide the parchment with the cookies over it to the wire rack; allow it to cool down totally.

Nutrition Information

- Calories: 101 calories;
- Cholesterol: 4
- Protein: 1.5
- Total Fat: 5.4
- Sodium: 26
- Total Carbohydrate: 12

20. Chocolate Peanut Butter Blossoms

Serving: 16 | Prep: 20mins | Ready in:

Ingredients

- 1/2 cup shortening
- 1/2 cup white sugar
- 1/2 cup brown sugar
- 1/2 cup peanut butter
- 1 egg
- 2 tablespoons milk
- 1 teaspoon vanilla extract
- 1 1/2 cups all-purpose flour
- 1 teaspoon baking soda
- 1/2 teaspoon salt
- 1/4 cup white sugar, or as needed
- 48 milk chocolate candy kisses (such as Hershey's Kisses®), unwrapped

Direction

- Preheat the oven to 375°F (190°C).
- In a large bowl, beat together the vanilla extract, milk, egg, peanut butter, brown sugar, 1/2 cup white sugar and shortening with an electric mixer until mixture is creamy.
- In a bowl, whisk salt, baking powder and flour together. Stir the dry mixture into peanut butter mixture.
- Pour 1/4 cup white sugar into a shallow bowl. Wrap about 1-1/2 teaspoons of dough over 1 chocolate kiss and form into a ball. Roll dough ball in sugar until coated. Arrange dough balls on baking sheets 1-1/2 inches apart.
- Bake in preheated oven for about 6 minutes or until cookies is set and chocolate softened. Immediately press cookies with the bottom of a glass to flatten them.

Nutrition Information

- Calories: 288 calories;
- Total Fat: 15.2
- Sodium: 209
- Total Carbohydrate: 35.3
- Cholesterol: 15
- Protein: 4.6

21. Chocolate Peanut Butter Cookies

Serving: 48 | Prep: 25mins | Ready in:

Ingredients

- 2 1/2 cups rolled oats
- 1 cup all-purpose flour
- 1 cup unsweetened cocoa powder
- 1 teaspoon baking powder
- 1 teaspoon baking soda
- 1/2 teaspoon salt
- 3/4 cup unsalted butter, at room temperature
- 1/2 cup milk
- 1/4 cup peanut butter
- 1 cup white sugar
- 1 cup brown sugar
- 2 eggs
- 2 teaspoons vanilla extract
- 1 (10 ounce) package peanut butter chips

Direction

- Pulse oats till oats look like flour in food processor/blender. Put oats in big bowl; mix salt, baking soda, baking powder, cocoa powder and flour in.
- Beat brown sugar, white sugar, peanut butter, milk and butter till fluffy and light in another bowl. One by one, beat eggs in; let each egg blend into butter mixture prior to adding next. With last egg, beat vanilla extract in; mix oat mixture in till blended well. Fold peanut butter chips in; mix just enough to combine evenly; refrigerate the dough for 30 minutes.
- Preheat an oven to 175°C/350°F.

- Drop 1-in. spoonfuls dough on ungreased baking sheets, 2-in. apart.
- In preheated oven, bake for 10-12 minutes till cookie middles are set.

Nutrition Information

- Calories: 132 calories;
- Total Fat: 5.9
- Sodium: 87
- Total Carbohydrate: 17.6
- Cholesterol: 16
- Protein: 3.1

22. Chocolate Peanut Butter Date Bars

Serving: 24 | Prep: | Ready in:

Ingredients

- 3/4 cup butter
- 1 cup semisweet chocolate chips
- 1 1/3 cups all-purpose flour
- 1/4 cup white sugar
- 1/2 teaspoon baking powder
- 3/4 cup confectioners' sugar
- 2 eggs
- 3/4 cup creamy peanut butter
- 3/4 cup dates, pitted and chopped
- 3/4 cup finely chopped walnuts
- 2 tablespoons water
- 1 tablespoon shortening

Direction

- Preheat an oven to 350°F then grease 9x13-in. pan.
- Melt 1/2 cup chocolate chips and 1/2 cup butter in saucepan on low heat.
- Take off heat. Add sugar and flour; stir well. Firmly press mixture in greased pan; bake it for 10 minutes.

- Meanwhile, mix baking powder and confectioners' sugar in mixing bowl.
- Add water, walnuts, dates, peanut butter, leftover 1/4 cup butter and eggs; thoroughly mix.
- Cool baked crust for 5 minutes; spread date mixture on crust. Bake till golden for 15-20 minutes.
- Melt 1 tbsp. shortening and leftover 1/2 cup chocolate chips; spread on filling and baked crust. Sprinkle extra chopped nuts if desired. Completely cool; cut to bars.

Nutrition Information

- Calories: 227 calories;
- Total Fat: 15.3
- Sodium: 95
- Total Carbohydrate: 21.1
- Cholesterol: 31
- Protein: 4.3

23. Chocolate Peanut Butter Dreams

Serving: 48 | Prep: | Ready in:

Ingredients

- 1 1/2 cups packed brown sugar
- 1 cup peanut butter
- 3/4 cup butter, softened
- 1/3 cup water
- 1 egg
- 1 teaspoon vanilla extract
- 3 cups rolled oats
- 1 1/2 cups all-purpose flour
- 1/2 teaspoon baking soda
- 1 1/2 cups semisweet chocolate chips
- 4 tablespoons shortening
- 1/3 cup chopped peanuts

Direction

- Preheat an oven to 175°C/350°F.
- Beat margarine/butter, peanut butter and sugar till fluffy; blend vanilla, egg and water in.
- Mix baking soda, flour and oats; add to mixture.
- Form to 1-in. balls; put on ungreased cookie sheet. Use glass dipped in sugar to flatten; bake for 8-10 minutes. Fully cool.
- Melt shortening and chocolate in saucepan on low heat; mix till smooth. Get 1/2 tsp., and spread on each cookie, sprinkle with nuts. Chill till set.

Nutrition Information

- Calories: 159 calories;
- Cholesterol: 12
- Protein: 3
- Total Fat: 9.2
- Sodium: 63
- Total Carbohydrate: 17.8

24. Chocolate Peanut Butter Squares

Serving: 18 | Prep: | Ready in:

Ingredients

- 1 cup butter
- 4 cups confectioners' sugar
- 2 cups peanut butter
- 1 1/2 cups graham cracker crumbs
- 1/2 cup butter
- 1 cup semisweet chocolate chips

Direction

- Melt 1 cup margarine/butter on low heat; take off heat. Mix graham cracker crumbs, peanut butter and confectioners' sugar in. Spread mixture in jellyroll pan; evenly pat down.

- Topping: Melt 1 cup chocolate chips and 1/2 cup margarine/butter; spread mixture on peanut butter mixture. Refrigerate for 30 minutes then cut to squares.

Nutrition Information

- Calories: 482 calories;
- Total Carbohydrate: 43.4
- Cholesterol: 41
- Protein: 8.2
- Total Fat: 33.3
- Sodium: 284

25. Classic Peanut Butter Cookies

Serving: 24 | Prep: 15mins | Ready in:

Ingredients

- 1 cup unsalted butter
- 1 cup crunchy peanut butter
- 1 cup white sugar
- 1 cup packed brown sugar
- 2 eggs
- 2 1/2 cups all-purpose flour
- 1 teaspoon baking powder
- 1/2 teaspoon salt
- 1 1/2 teaspoons baking soda

Direction

- In a bowl, cream sugars, peanut butter and butter; whip in eggs.
- Sift salt, baking soda, baking powder, and flour in another bowl; mix into butter mixture. Add dough into the refrigerator for 60 minutes.
- Roll dough into 1 inch balls and place onto baking sheets. Flatten each ball using a fork, creating a crisscross pattern. Bake for roughly 10 minutes till cookies start to brown in a preheated 375pF oven.

Nutrition Information

- Calories: 252 calories;
- Protein: 4.5
- Total Fat: 13.6
- Sodium: 209
- Total Carbohydrate: 29.7
- Cholesterol: 36

26. College Munchies (Edible Chocolate Peanut Butter Cookie Dough)

Serving: 12 | Prep: 15mins | Ready in:

Ingredients

- 2/3 cup white sugar
- 3 tablespoons peanut butter
- 3 tablespoons margarine, at room temperature
- 1/3 cup instant milk chocolate drink mix
- 1 tablespoon milk, or as needed
- 3 cups all-purpose flour, or as needed

Direction

- Beat margarine, peanut butter and sugar till creamy in big bowl; mix milk and chocolate drink mix in till blended. Mix flour in till dough isn't sticky and comes together.
- Roll dough to balls; put on waxed paper-lined big plate. Keep in the fridge.

Nutrition Information

- Calories: 214 calories;
- Total Fat: 5.1
- Sodium: 55
- Total Carbohydrate: 37.8
- Cholesterol: 1
- Protein: 4.4

27. Cookie Butter Cookies

Serving: 25 | Prep: 15mins | Ready in:

Ingredients

- 3/4 cup butter, softened
- 3/4 cup brown sugar
- 3/4 cup white sugar
- 1/2 cup cookie butter
- 1/2 cup peanut butter
- 2 cups all-purpose flour
- 1 egg
- 1/2 teaspoon baking soda
- 1/2 teaspoon baking powder
- 1/4 teaspoon salt
- 1/3 cup white sugar

Direction

- Preheat oven to 175°C or 350°F. Use parchment paper to line one baking sheet.
- In a big bowl, using an electric mixer to whip three quarters cup of white sugar, brown sugar and butter till becomes smooth in texture. Put in peanut butter and cookie butter; whip till becomes fluffy. Stir salt, baking powder, baking soda, egg and flour into the butter mixture making cookie dough. Roll the dough to have teaspoon-sized balls.
- Spread a third cup of sugar to a shallow plate. Roll dough balls into the sugar to coat and arrange to the prepped baking sheet. Press dough balls using a fork two times to flatten a bit and press a crosshatch shape into the cookies top.
- Bake for roughly 12 minutes in the preheated oven till turns golden brown.

Nutrition Information

- Calories: 196 calories;
- Sodium: 125
- Total Carbohydrate: 24
- Cholesterol: 22
- Protein: 2.6
- Total Fat: 10.2

28. Crunchy Peanut Butter Swirl Brownies

Serving: 36 | Prep: | Ready in:

Ingredients

- 1 (3 ounce) package cream cheese, softened
- 1/3 cup peanut butter
- 1/4 cup white sugar
- 1 egg
- 1/2 cup chopped peanuts
- 1 (19.8 ounce) package brownie mix
- 2 tablespoons water
- 1/2 cup vegetable oil
- 2 eggs

Direction

- Heat an oven to 175°C/350°F then grease bottom of 1 13x9-in. pan.
- Beat 1 egg, white sugar, peanut butter and cream cheese on medium speed till smooth in small bowl. Mix peanuts in; put aside.
- Beat 2 eggs, oil, water and brownie mix with wooden spoon for 50 strokes in big bowl.
- Spread 1/2 batter in prepped pan; by tablespoonfuls, drop filling on brownie batter. Put leftover batter on filling; pull knife through batter in wide curves and turn pan. Repeat to get marbled effect.
- Bake for 30 minutes at 175°C/350°F. Completely cool; cut to bars. Keep in the fridge, tightly covered.

Nutrition Information

- Calories: 139 calories;
- Total Fat: 8.8
- Sodium: 71
- Total Carbohydrate: 14.2
- Cholesterol: 18
- Protein: 2.4

29. Dad's Favorite Peanut Butter Cookies

Serving: 36 | Prep: 10mins | Ready in:

Ingredients

- 1/2 cup shortening
- 1/2 cup crunchy peanut butter
- 1/2 cup white sugar
- 1/2 cup packed brown sugar
- 1 egg
- 1 1/4 cups all-purpose flour
- 3/4 teaspoon baking soda
- 1/2 teaspoon baking powder
- 1/4 teaspoon salt

Direction

- Cream sugars, peanut butter and shortening; beat egg in. Mix salt, baking powder, baking soda and flour then mix into peanut butter mixture slowly. Cover; refrigerate dough for no less than 1 hour.
- Preheat an oven to 190°C/375°F. Make small dough balls; use fork dipped in water to flatten to make crosswise pattern.
- In preheated oven, bake for 10-12 minutes till just set. Transfer from baking sheets to wire racks; cool.

Nutrition Information

- Calories: 86 calories;
- Sodium: 69
- Total Carbohydrate: 9.9
- Cholesterol: 5
- Protein: 1.5
- Total Fat: 4.8

30. Delicious Peanut Butter Cookies

Serving: 48 | Prep: 10mins | Ready in:

Ingredients

- 1/2 cup shortening
- 1 1/4 cups packed light brown sugar
- 3/4 cup peanut butter
- 1 egg
- 3 tablespoons milk
- 1 tablespoon vanilla extract
- 1 3/4 cups all-purpose flour
- 3/4 teaspoon baking soda
- 3/4 teaspoon salt

Direction

- Preheat the oven to 190 degrees C or 375 degrees F.
- Cream peanut butter, brown sugar and shortening in a medium-sized bowl till become smooth in consistency. Mix in vanilla, milk and egg. . Mix salt, baking soda and flour together; mix into the peanut butter mixture till well blended. Drop by rounded spoonfuls to the ungreased cookie sheets.
- Bake in the preheated oven for 8 - 10 minutes. Let cookies cool down on the baking sheet for 5 minutes prior to removing to a wire rack to let it cool down totally.

Nutrition Information

- Calories: 84 calories;
- Total Fat: 4.3
- Sodium: 78
- Total Carbohydrate: 10
- Cholesterol: 4
- Protein: 1.7

31. Double Peanut Butter Cookies I

Serving: 24 | Prep: | Ready in:

Ingredients

- 1 1/2 cups sifted all-purpose flour
- 1 tablespoon milk
- 1/2 cup white sugar
- 1/2 teaspoon baking soda
- 1/4 cup light corn syrup
- 1/4 teaspoon salt
- 1/2 cup shortening
- 1 cup peanut butter
- 1 cup semisweet chocolate chips

Direction

- Mix salt, soda, sugar and flour; cut peanut butter and shortening in till it looks like coarse meal. Blend milk and syrup in.
- Form to 2-in. diameter roll then chill; cut to 1/8-1/4-in. thick.
- Put 1/2 slices onto ungreased cookie sheet; spread 1/2 tsp. peanut butter on each. Sprinkle chocolate chips over peanut butter. Use leftover cookie slices to cover; use fork to seal edges.
- Use leftover cookie slices to cover; use fork to seal edges. Bake for 12 minutes at 175°C/350°F till browned.

Nutrition Information

- Calories: 189 calories;
- Total Fat: 11.9
- Sodium: 103
- Total Carbohydrate: 19.3
- Cholesterol: 1
- Protein: 3.8

32. Double Peanut Butter Cookies II

Serving: 60 | Prep: | Ready in:

Ingredients

- 2 1/2 cups whole wheat flour
- 2 cups pastry flour
- 1 1/2 teaspoons baking powder
- 1/2 teaspoon salt
- 1/2 cup vegetable oil
- 2 cups peanut butter
- 1 1/2 cups honey
- 3 tablespoons plain yogurt
- 1/2 cup peanut butter

Direction

- Sift salt, baking powder, pastry flour and whole wheat flour; put aside. Mix yogurt, honey, 2 cups peanut butter and vegetable oil till smooth in medium bowl. Add dry ingredients; mix by hand till blended well. Form to 2-in. diameter roll; wrap. Chill till firm.
- Preheat an oven to 175°C/350°F.
- Unwrap dough roll; cut to 1/4-in. slices. Put 1/2 cookies on unprepped baking sheet. Spread 1/2 tsp. peanut butter on middle of every cookie on sheets. Use leftover cookie rounds to cover; tightly seal edges with fork.
- In preheated oven, bake for 10-12 minutes. Transfer cookies from baking sheets to wire racks; cool.

Nutrition Information

- Calories: 136 calories;
- Sodium: 82
- Total Carbohydrate: 15.8
- Cholesterol: 1
- Protein: 3.8
- Total Fat: 7.4

33. Doubly Delicious Peanut Butter Cookies

Serving: 18 | Prep: | Ready in:

Ingredients

- 1 cup white sugar
- 1 cup packed brown sugar
- 1 cup crunchy peanut butter
- 1/2 cup butter flavored shortening
- 2 eggs
- 1 1/2 cups all-purpose flour
- 1/2 teaspoon baking soda
- 1/4 teaspoon salt
- 2 cups peanut butter chips

Direction

- Preheat an oven to 175°C/350°F.
- Beat shortening, peanut butter and sugars on medium speed till blended well in big bowl. One by one, add eggs; beat well after each. Mix salt, baking soda and flour; at low speed, slowly add to creamed mixture. Mix till just blended. Use spoon to mix peanut butter chips in; it will be stiff.
- Form to 1 1/2-in. balls; put on ungreased baking sheet, 2-in. apart. Use floured fork tines to create crisscross marks on top.
- Bake till tops are moist and edges are set for 8-10 minutes; cool on baking sheet for 8 minutes. Transfer to flat surface.

Nutrition Information

- Calories: 423 calories;
- Total Carbohydrate: 47.4
- Cholesterol: 21
- Protein: 10.9
- Total Fat: 21.3
- Sodium: 214

34. Easy Chocolate Drops

Serving: 18 | Prep: | Ready in:

Ingredients

- 3 tablespoons margarine
- 3 tablespoons peanut butter

- 1 cup semisweet chocolate chips
- 3 cups whole wheat flake cereal

Direction

- Mix chocolate chips, peanut butter and margarine in a medium-sized saucepan. Cook on low heat, while mixing often till becomes melted. Take out of the heat and mix in cereal. Drop by spoonfuls onto wax paper or the greased cookie sheets, and keep chilled in the refrigerator till becomes set.

Nutrition Information

- Calories: 95 calories;
- Protein: 1.6
- Total Fat: 6.1
- Sodium: 69
- Total Carbohydrate: 10.5
- Cholesterol: 0

35. Easy Peanut Butter Cookies

Serving: 60 | Prep: | Ready in:

Ingredients

- 1 (14 ounce) can sweetened condensed milk
- 3/4 cup peanut butter
- 1 egg
- 1 teaspoon vanilla extract
- 2 cups buttermilk baking mix
- 1/2 cup white sugar

Direction

- Preheat an oven to 175°C/350°F.
- Beat vanilla, egg, peanut butter and condensed milk till smooth in big bowl. Add biscuit mix; stir well. Chill for 1 hour minimum.
- Form dough to 1-in. balls then roll balls in sugar; put on ungreased baking sheets, 2-in. apart. Use fork to slightly flatten balls.

- Bake till lightly browned for 6-8 minutes, don't overbake; cool. Keep at room temperature in tightly covered container.

Nutrition Information

- Calories: 61 calories;
- Cholesterol: 5
- Protein: 1.8
- Total Fat: 2.3
- Sodium: 101
- Total Carbohydrate: 8.8

36. Easy Peanut Butter Fudge

Serving: 24 | Prep: | Ready in:

Ingredients

- 1 pound confectioners' sugar
- 1/2 cup peanut butter
- 1/2 cup unsweetened cocoa powder
- 6 tablespoons milk
- 2 teaspoons vanilla extract

Direction

- Line wax paper on an 8x8-inch square pan
- Combine vanilla, milk, cocoa, peanut butter and confectioner's sugar; mix until mixture is smooth. Refrigerate until hardened, cut into squares.
- Preheat the oven to 350°F (180°C).
- Beat margarine, peanut butter and brown sugar until the mixture is fluffy.
- Blend in vanilla, egg and water.
- Add combined baking soda, flour and oats; mix properly. Chill, with cover for 1 hour.
- Form into 1 inch balls. Arrange on ungreased cookie sheet. Press each ball into 1/4-inch thick circles using a sugar-coated glass bottom.
- Bake until edges turn golden brown, for 8 to 10 minutes. Transfer to wire racks, completely cool.

- For frosting: In a saucepan, melt chocolate over low heat. Stir in vegetable shortening, mix until smooth.
- Place 1/2 teaspoon melted chocolate on top of every cookie. Sprinkle chopped peanuts on top, refrigerate until set. Store in an airtight container.

Nutrition Information

- Calories: 112 calories;
- Total Fat: 3
- Sodium: 27
- Total Carbohydrate: 21.1
- Cholesterol: 1
- Protein: 1.8

37. Easy, Chewy Flourless Peanut Butter Cookies

Serving: 12 | Prep: 10mins | Ready in:

Ingredients

- 1 cup peanut butter
- 1/2 cup white sugar
- 1/3 cup packed brown sugar
- 1 egg
- 1 teaspoon vanilla extract
- 1/2 teaspoon baking soda
- 1/2 cup semisweet chocolate chips (optional)

Direction

- Preheat an oven to 175°C/350°F.
- Use electric mixer to beat brown sugar, white sugar and peanut butter till smooth in big bowl. Mix baking soda, vanilla extract and egg into peanut butter mixture; mix chocolate chips in.
- By small rounded spoonfuls, drop mixture on baking sheet, 2-in. apart.
- In preheated oven, bake for 8 minutes till cookies are golden and flattened.

Nutrition Information

- Calories: 222 calories;
- Sodium: 159
- Total Carbohydrate: 23
- Cholesterol: 16
- Protein: 6.2
- Total Fat: 13.3

38. Eggless Peanut Butter Cookies

Serving: 24 | Prep: | Ready in:

Ingredients

- 1 cup shortening
- 1 cup creamy peanut butter
- 1 cup white sugar
- 1 cup packed brown sugar
- 1/2 cup buttermilk
- 2 1/2 cups all-purpose flour
- 1 teaspoon baking powder
- 1 1/2 teaspoons baking soda
- 1/2 teaspoon salt

Direction

- Preheat an oven to 190°C/375°F then grease cookie sheet lightly.
- Mix buttermilk, brown sugar, white sugar, peanut butter and shortening till fully combined and smooth.
- Add salt, baking soda, baking powder and flour to peanut butter mixture; mix till blended well.
- Drop cookies on lightly grease cookie sheet, 2-in. apart. Use fork dipped in flour to flatten; bake for 10-12 minutes at 190°C/375°F.

Nutrition Information

- Calories: 255 calories;
- Cholesterol: 1

- Protein: 4.2
- Total Fat: 14.1
- Sodium: 205
- Total Carbohydrate: 29.7

39. Elaine's Peanut Butter Cookies

Serving: 36 | Prep: 10mins | Ready in:

Ingredients

- 1 (18.25 ounce) package yellow cake mix
- 1 cup creamy peanut butter
- 1/2 cup vegetable oil
- 2 eggs
- 2 tablespoons water

Direction

- Preheat an oven to 175°C/350°F.
- Put cake mix in big bowl; create well in middle. Add water, eggs, oil and peanut butter; mix till blended well. By teaspoonfuls, drop on ungreased cookie sheets. Use fork dipped in water to slightly flatten.
- In preheated oven, bake for 10-12 minutes; set cookies for 2-3 minutes on cookie sheet. Transfer from cookie sheet to wire racks; cool.

Nutrition Information

- Calories: 135 calories;
- Protein: 2.8
- Total Fat: 8.6
- Sodium: 131
- Total Carbohydrate: 12.6
- Cholesterol: 11

40. Elvis Cookies

Serving: 24 | Prep: 15mins | Ready in:

Ingredients

- 1 cup butter, softened
- 2 cups brown sugar
- 1 cup white sugar
- 1 1/2 cups peanut butter
- 2 teaspoons vanilla extract
- 3 ripe bananas
- 2 1/2 cups all-purpose flour
- 1/2 teaspoon baking powder

Direction

- Set the oven to 175°C or 350°F to preheat. Grease a baking sheet lightly.
- In a bowl, stir together vanilla, peanut butter, white sugar, brown sugar and butter. Mash into the mixture with bananas until there are several of lumps remained. In, a separate bowl, sift baking powder and flour together, then put into the banana mixture and stir until blended completely. Drop mixture onto prepped baking sheet by rounded tablespoons.
- In the preheated oven, bake for around 10 minutes, until firm and browned slightly.

Nutrition Information

- Calories: 326 calories;
- Sodium: 144
- Total Carbohydrate: 42.9
- Cholesterol: 20
- Protein: 5.7
- Total Fat: 16

41. Favorite Chocolate Peanut Butter Cookies

Serving: 36 | Prep: 15mins | Ready in:

Ingredients

- 1/2 cup butter

- 1/4 cup vegetable shortening
- 1 cup white sugar
- 1/2 cup brown sugar
- 2 eggs
- 1 1/2 teaspoons vanilla extract
- 2 cups all-purpose flour
- 1 teaspoon baking powder
- 1/4 cup unsweetened cocoa powder
- 1/8 teaspoon salt
- 1 (12 ounce) package peanut butter chips

Direction

- Preheat an oven to 175°C/350°F.
- Use electric mixer to beat brown sugar, white sugar, shortening and butter till smooth in big bowl; beat 1st egg into butter till blended completely. Beat vanilla and 2nd egg in. Mix salt, cocoa powder, baking powder and flour in separate bowl; mix flour mixture into butter mixture just till incorporated. Fold peanut butter chips in; mix just enough to combine evenly.
- Drop dough spoonfuls on ungreased baking sheets, 2-in. apart.
- In preheated oven, bake for 8 minutes till cookies are set.

Nutrition Information

- Calories: 149 calories;
- Cholesterol: 17
- Protein: 3.1
- Total Fat: 6.9
- Sodium: 67
- Total Carbohydrate: 18.6

42. Favorite Peanut Butter Cookies

Serving: 54 | Prep: 30mins | Ready in:

Ingredients

- 1 1/4 cups creamy peanut butter

- 1 cup margarine
- 3/4 cup white sugar
- 3/4 cup packed light brown sugar
- 2 eggs
- 1/2 teaspoon vanilla extract
- 2 1/4 cups all-purpose flour
- 1 teaspoon baking powder
- 1 teaspoon baking soda

Direction

- Preheat an oven to 190°C/375°F.
- Cream white sugar, brown sugar, margarine and peanut butter in big bowl; beat vanilla and eggs in. Mix baking soda, baking powder and flour; mix into peanut butter mixture. Shape dough to walnut-sized balls; put on ungreased cookie sheets, 2-in. apart. Dip fork into flour; slightly flatten each cookie with crisscross.
- In preheated oven, bake for 12-15 minutes till just lightly browned. Cool cookies for 5 minutes on baking sheet; transfer to wire rack to completely cool.

Nutrition Information

- Calories: 109 calories;
- Sodium: 100
- Total Carbohydrate: 11
- Cholesterol: 7
- Protein: 2.3
- Total Fat: 6.6

43. Flourless Peanut Butter Cookies

Serving: 6 | Prep: | Ready in:

Ingredients

- 1 cup peanut butter
- 1 cup white sugar
- 1 egg

Direction

- Preheat oven to 180 degrees C or 350 degrees F
- Mix the ingredients and drop by teaspoonfuls onto the cookie sheet. Bake for 8 minutes. Allow to cool down. Double the recipe as you wish because the recipe doesn't make a big amount.

Nutrition Information

- Calories: 394 calories;
- Total Fat: 22.5
- Sodium: 209
- Total Carbohydrate: 41.8
- Cholesterol: 31
- Protein: 11.8

---

44. Ginger Touched Oatmeal Peanut Butter Cookies

Serving: 12 | Prep: | Ready in:

Ingredients

- 1/2 cup butter
- 1/2 cup shortening
- 1 cup peanut butter
- 1 cup packed brown sugar
- 3/4 cup white sugar
- 2 eggs
- 1/2 teaspoon vanilla extract
- 1 1/2 cups all-purpose flour
- 2 teaspoons baking soda
- 1 teaspoon salt
- 1 teaspoon ground ginger
- 1 cup rolled oats
- 1 cup chopped crystallized ginger

Direction

- Preheat an oven to 175°C/350°F.
- Cream white sugar, brown sugar, butter and shortening in medium bowl; beat vanilla, peanut butter and eggs in. Mix ground ginger, salt, baking soda and flour; mix into creamed

mixture. Mix candied ginger and rolled oats in; by rounded teaspoonfuls, drop onto unprepped cookie sheet.

- In preheated oven, bake for 10-12 minutes till golden brown. Transfer from baking sheets onto wire racks. When cool, keep in airtight container.

Nutrition Information

- Calories: 509 calories;
- Cholesterol: 51
- Protein: 9.1
- Total Fat: 28.5
- Sodium: 579
- Total Carbohydrate: 57.9

---

45. Gluten Free Peanut Butter Cookies

Serving: 15 | Prep: 30mins | Ready in:

Ingredients

- 2 cups peanut butter
- 2 cups white sugar
- 4 eggs, beaten
- 2 cups semi-sweet chocolate chips (optional)
- 1 1/2 cups chopped pecans (optional)

Direction

- Preheat an oven to 175°C/350°F then grease cookie sheet.
- Mix sugar, eggs and peanut butter till smooth; mix nuts (optional) and chocolate chips in. By tablespoonfuls, put dough on cookie sheet.
- Bake till lightly browned for 10-12 minutes; cool cookies for 5-10 minutes on cookie sheets then remove.

Nutrition Information

- Calories: 513 calories;

- Cholesterol: 50
- Protein: 12.9
- Total Fat: 33
- Sodium: 177
- Total Carbohydrate: 49.6

46. Grad Cap Cookies

Serving: 50 | Prep: 1hours | Ready in:

Ingredients

- 10 (4 inch) pieces pull-apart red string licorice (such as Twizzlers®)
- 50 miniature chocolate covered peanut butter cups, unwrapped
- 1 cup prepared chocolate frosting
- 50 chocolate-covered graham cracker cookies
- 50 candy-coated milk chocolate pieces (such as M's®) (optional)

Direction

- Slice licorice candy whips to 2-in. pieces; pull apart to create small strings then put aside.
- Put miniature peanut butter cup on work surface, upside down; top with dab of frosting then center chocolate-covered graham cracker cookie on frosting to create small cap with mortarboard. Press cookie gently onto peanut butter cup.
- Put small frosting dab on middle of graham cracker cookie; attach red licorice string for tassel and let tassel drape on cookie edge. Put candy-coated milk chocolate piece on middle of cookie on tassel's end to create button.
- Repeat with leftover cookies and candies to create 50 graduation caps with tassels.

Nutrition Information

- Calories: 151 calories;
- Total Fat: 6.9
- Sodium: 79

- Total Carbohydrate: 21.6
- Cholesterol: 1
- Protein: 1.8

47. Grain Free Peanut Butter Cookies

Serving: 12 | Prep: 10mins | Ready in:

Ingredients

- 3/4 cup flaxseed meal
- 1/2 cup coconut flour
- 2 teaspoons baking powder
- 1 teaspoon ground cinnamon
- 1 teaspoon salt
- 1 cup peanut butter
- 2/3 cup unsweetened applesauce
- 2 eggs
- 1/4 cup butter, melted
- 1 teaspoon vanilla extract

Direction

- Preheat an oven to 200°C/400°F.
- Whisk salt, cinnamon, baking powder, coconut flour and flaxseed meal in bowl. Mix vanilla extract, eggs, butter, applesauce and peanut butter in another bowl; stir into flaxseed meal mixture till dough just mixes. Put dough on baking sheet; use wet fork to press into every cookie to flatten.
- In preheated oven, bake for 10-15 minutes till cookies brown lightly.

Nutrition Information

- Calories: 217 calories;
- Total Fat: 18.5
- Sodium: 415
- Total Carbohydrate: 8.2
- Cholesterol: 41
- Protein: 7.8

48. Healthier Classic Peanut Butter Cookies

Serving: 24 | Prep: 10mins | Ready in:

Ingredients

- 1/2 cup unsalted butter
- 1 cup crunchy peanut butter
- 1/4 cup applesauce
- 1 cup white sugar
- 1 cup packed brown sugar
- 4 egg whites
- 2 1/2 cups all-purpose flour
- 1 teaspoon baking powder
- 1 1/2 teaspoons baking soda

Direction

- Preheat oven to 190 degrees C or 375 degrees F.
- In a big bowl, using an electric mixer to beat brown sugar, white sugar, applesauce, peanut butter and butter till becomes smooth. Put in eggs and whip till smooth.
- In another bowl, sift baking soda, baking powder and flour; mix into peanut butter batter. Add batter into the refrigerator for 60 minutes.
- Roll dough into the walnut-sized balls and add 2 inches apart to the ungreased baking sheets. Flatten each ball using a fork, shaping a crisscross pattern.
- Bake for roughly 10 minutes till cookies starts to brown in the preheated oven.

Nutrition Information

- Calories: 216 calories;
- Total Fat: 9.3
- Sodium: 164
- Total Carbohydrate: 30
- Cholesterol: 10
- Protein: 4.6

49. High Protein Peanut Butter Balls

Serving: 25 | Prep: 20mins | Ready in:

Ingredients

- 2 cups crunchy peanut butter
- 2 scoops cocoa whey protein powder
- 2 ripe bananas, mashed
- 2 tablespoons flax seeds

Direction

- Mix flaxseed, bananas, cocoa whey powder and peanut butter in big bowl.
- Mold mixture to walnut-sized balls; put in parchment-lined container to separate the layers then freeze before serving for minimum of 2 hours.

Nutrition Information

- Calories: 136 calories;
- Protein: 5.3
- Total Fat: 10.8
- Sodium: 102
- Total Carbohydrate: 7
- Cholesterol: 1

50. Honey Wheat Cookies

Serving: 48 | Prep: 15mins | Ready in:

Ingredients

- 1/2 cup butter or margarine, softened
- 1/2 cup natural peanut butter
- 1/2 cup honey
- 1 egg
- 1 tablespoon vanilla extract
- 1 cup sifted whole wheat flour
- 1/2 cup dry milk powder

- 1/2 cup wheat bran
- 1 teaspoon baking soda

Direction

- Preheat an oven to 175°C/350°F.
- Mix peanut butter and butter till smooth in medium bowl; mix vanilla, egg and honey in. Mix baking soda, wheat bran, dry milk powder and whole wheat flour; mix into peanut butter mixture. By teaspoonfuls, drop on ungreased baking sheets.
- In preheated oven, bake for 8-10 minutes till edges start to brown. Transfer from baking sheet to wire racks; cool.

Nutrition Information

- Calories: 63 calories;
- Sodium: 54
- Total Carbohydrate: 6.3
- Cholesterol: 10
- Protein: 1.6
- Total Fat: 3.9

51. JIF® Irresistible Peanut Butter Cookies

Serving: 24 | Prep: | Ready in:

Ingredients

- 1 1/4 cups firmly packed light brown sugar
- 3/4 cup JIF® Peanut Butter
- 1/2 cup Butter Flavor CRISCO® Stick
- 3 tablespoons milk
- 1 tablespoon vanilla
- 1 egg
- 1 3/4 cups sifted all-purpose flour
- 3/4 teaspoon baking soda
- 3/4 teaspoon salt

Direction

- Preheat oven to 375°F. Add sheets of foil over countertop to cool cookies.
- In a big bowl, mix vanilla, milk, shortening, JIF® peanut butter and brown sugar. Whip on medium speed in an electric mixer till well blended. Put in egg. Whip just till blended.
- Mix salt, baking soda and flour. Pour into the creamed mixture on low speed. Stir till just blended.
- Drop by rounded tablespoonfuls 2 inches apart to the ungreased cookie sheet. Flatten a bit in crisscross pattern using tines of fork.
- Bake the baking sheet once at a time till just starts to brown and set for 7 to 8 minutes. Avoid over baking. Let it cool down for 2 minutes on the baking sheet. Take the cookies out to the foil to cool down totally.

Nutrition Information

- Calories: 166 calories;
- Sodium: 157
- Total Carbohydrate: 20.1
- Cholesterol: 8
- Protein: 3.3
- Total Fat: 8.3

52. Jennah's Famous Peanut Butter Blossoms

Serving: 30 | Prep: 20mins | Ready in:

Ingredients

- 2 cups baking mix (such as Bisquick ®)
- 1 (14 ounce) can sweetened condensed milk (such as Eagle Brand®)
- 3/4 cup peanut butter (such as Jif®)
- 1 teaspoon vanilla extract
- 1/4 cup white sugar, or as needed
- 30 unwrapped milk chocolate candy kisses (such as Hershey's Kisses®), or as needed

Direction

- Preheat an oven to 175°C/350°F.
- Mix vanilla extract, peanut butter, sweetened condensed milk and baking mix in bowl; roll dough to 1-in. balls.
- Put sugar on plate then roll balls in sugar till fully coated; put on baking sheet.
- In preheated oven, bake for 8 minutes till edges are lightly browned. Press candy kiss in middle of each cookie. Put cookies on wire rack; cool.

Nutrition Information

- Calories: 144 calories;
- Total Fat: 7
- Sodium: 151
- Total Carbohydrate: 17.8
- Cholesterol: 5
- Protein: 3.5

53. Joey's Peanut Butter Cookies

Serving: 36 | Prep: 15mins | Ready in:

Ingredients

- 1 cup peanut butter
- 1/2 cup butter, softened
- 1/2 cup white sugar
- 1/2 cup packed brown sugar
- 1 egg
- 3 tablespoons milk
- 1 teaspoon vanilla extract
- 1 1/4 cups all-purpose flour
- 3/4 teaspoon baking powder
- 1/4 teaspoon salt

Direction

- Preheat an oven to 190°C/375°F.
- Cream brown sugar, white sugar, butter and peanut butter till blended in big bowl; one by one, beat vanilla, milk and egg in. Mix salt, baking powder and flour; mix into creamed

mixture. Roll tbsp. of dough to balls; put cookies on ungreased cookie sheets, 2-in. apart. Use fork tines to press each ball once.
- In preheated oven, bake for 8-10 minutes till edges are lightly browned.

Nutrition Information

- Calories: 106 calories;
- Total Carbohydrate: 10.6
- Cholesterol: 12
- Protein: 2.5
- Total Fat: 6.4
- Sodium: 81

54. Light And Soft Peanut Butter Cookies

Serving: 24 | Prep: 20mins | Ready in:

Ingredients

- 1 1/3 cups all-purpose flour
- 1/2 teaspoon baking soda
- 1/4 teaspoon salt
- 1/2 cup unsalted butter
- 1/2 cup reduced-fat creamy peanut butter (such as Jif®)
- 1/2 cup reduced-fat crunchy peanut butter (such as (Jif®)
- 1 egg white
- 1/3 cup white sugar
- 1 egg
- 1/3 cup brown sugar

Direction

- Preheat an oven to 150°C/300°F. Sift salt, baking soda and flour in bowl.
- Beat crunchy peanut butter, crema peanut butter and butter till smooth in big bowl; beat white sugar and egg whites into butter mixture till smooth. Add brown sugar and whole egg; beat till smooth. Mix flour mixture

slowly into butter mixture till batter is mixed well.

- Roll dough to 1 1/4-in. balls. Put on ungreased baking sheets, 2-in. apart. Use fork to press balls to make crosshatch. On baking sheet, freeze cookie dough for 5-8 minutes till dough is firm.
- In preheated oven, bake for 15 minutes till cookies puff up. Cool for 10 minutes in pans. Transfer to wire rack; completely cool.

Nutrition Information

- Calories: 149 calories;
- Total Fat: 8.1
- Sodium: 141
- Total Carbohydrate: 16.1
- Cholesterol: 18
- Protein: 3.8

55. Low Carb Peanut Butter Cookies

Serving: 16 | Prep: 10mins | Ready in:

Ingredients

- 1 cup peanut butter
- 1 cup vanilla extract
- 1 cup white sugar substitute
- 1 large egg

Direction

- Set an oven to preheat to 175°C (350°F). Use a silicone baking mat (like Silpat (R)) to line a baking tray.
- In a bowl, mix together the egg, sugar substitute, vanilla extract and peanut butter. On the prepared baking tray, drop 16 spoonfuls of dough, 1 inch apart.
- Let it bake for about 12 minutes until set.

Nutrition Information

- Calories: 146 calories;
- Total Fat: 8.4
- Sodium: 80
- Total Carbohydrate: 13.5
- Cholesterol: 12
- Protein: 4.4

56. Magic Peanut Butter Middles

Serving: 15 | Prep: | Ready in:

Ingredients

- 1 1/2 cups all-purpose flour
- 1/2 cup unsweetened cocoa powder
- 1/2 teaspoon baking soda
- 1/2 cup white sugar
- 1/2 cup packed brown sugar
- 1/2 cup soft margarine
- 1/4 cup peanut butter
- 1 teaspoon vanilla extract
- 1 egg
- 3/4 cup confectioners' sugar
- 3/4 cup peanut butter

Direction

- Blend baking soda, cocoa and flour in a small bowl. Mix until ingredients are well blended.
- In a large bowl, beat 1/4 cup peanut butter, butter or margarine, brown and white sugars, until fluffy and light. Add egg and vanilla, beat. Stir in the flour mixture until mixed. Set aside.
- For the filling: Combine 3/4 cup peanut butter and confectioner's sugar. Blend properly.
- Roll filling into 30 1-inch balls. Cover your hands with flour and form about 1 tablespoon dough around 1 peanut butter ball for each cookie, covering the filling fully. Arrange dough balls on an ungreased cookie sheet 2 inches apart. Roll a glass dipped in white sugar over the dough balls.

- Bake for 7 to 9 minutes at 375°F (190°C). Cookies should be set and cracked slightly when they are done.

Nutrition Information

- Calories: 289 calories;
- Sodium: 199
- Total Carbohydrate: 34.4
- Cholesterol: 12
- Protein: 6.7
- Total Fat: 15.5

57. Make Ahead Cookie Mix

Serving: 24 | Prep: 15mins | Ready in:

Ingredients

- 1 1/2 cups butter
- 1 tablespoon salt
- 2 teaspoons baking powder
- 6 cups all-purpose flour

Direction

- Mix baking powder, salt and butter in big bowl; mix flour in slowly. Keep in the fridge in covered container for up to 4 weeks.

Nutrition Information

- Calories: 216 calories;
- Protein: 3.3
- Total Fat: 11.8
- Sodium: 414
- Total Carbohydrate: 24
- Cholesterol: 31

58. Make Ahead Peanut Butter Cookies

Serving: 12 | Prep: | Ready in:

Ingredients

- 2 cups Make Ahead Cookie Mix
- 1 cup packed brown sugar
- 1/3 cup shortening
- 1/2 cup peanut butter
- 1/2 teaspoon vanilla extract
- 1 egg

Direction

- Preheat oven to 190 degrees C or 375 degrees F
- Mix egg, vanilla, peanut butter, shortening, brown sugar with 2 cups Make Ahead Cookie Mix.
- Form dough into balls. Add dough onto the ungreased cookie sheets. Using a fork to flatten. Bake for 7 to 11 minutes.

Nutrition Information

- Calories: 190 calories;
- Total Fat: 11.5
- Sodium: 60
- Total Carbohydrate: 20.1
- Cholesterol: 16
- Protein: 3.2

59. Melt In Your Mouth Peanut Butter Cookies

Serving: 36 | Prep: | Ready in:

Ingredients

- 1 cup shortening
- 1 cup white sugar
- 1 cup packed brown sugar
- 1 cup peanut butter

- 2 eggs
- 2 tablespoons water
- 2 1/2 cups sifted all-purpose flour
- 1 teaspoon baking soda
- 1 teaspoon salt

Direction

- Preheat an oven to 190°C/375°F.
- Beat peanut butter, sugars and shortening till mixed well; beat water and egg in.
- Beat salt, baking soda and flour in slowly. Use cookie press to make cookies on ungreased baking sheet or roll to balls then use fingers/floured fork to smash flat.
- Bake for 12 minutes at 190°C/375° till done; puffed up cookie will lower down to level for 12 minutes or more till done. Before then it is more chewy.
- High altitude: Omit water. Add eggs last, stirring well yet not beating them like at sea level. Put temperature to 200°C/390°F/convection oven at 155°C/312°F for about 15 minutes.

Nutrition Information

- Calories: 173 calories;
- Sodium: 138
- Total Carbohydrate: 19.6
- Cholesterol: 10
- Protein: 3.1
- Total Fat: 9.7

60. Michelle's Peanut Butter Dots

Serving: 12 | Prep: | Ready in:

Ingredients

- 1 cup butter
- 1 cup white sugar
- 1 cup peanut butter
- 1/4 cup milk

- 1 teaspoon vanilla extract
- 2 cups all-purpose flour

Direction

- Combine vanilla, milk, peanut butter and sugar in a big mixing bowl. Use hand to mix for 3 minutes or until mixture is creamy.
- Mix flour thoroughly in to creamy mix. Form small dough balls by hand, about an-inch in diameter. Arrange about 3/4 inch apart on greased cookie sheet. Press fork on cookies to make criss cross pattern (this will make cookies flatten partially). Be careful not to over flatten dough, dough should not touch each other.
- Bake at 350°F (175°C) for 18 to 25 minutes.

Nutrition Information

- Calories: 406 calories;
- Total Fat: 26.5
- Sodium: 210
- Total Carbohydrate: 37.1
- Cholesterol: 41
- Protein: 7.9

61. Michelle's Peanut Butter Marbled Brownies

Serving: 36 | Prep: 20mins | Ready in:

Ingredients

- 2 (3 ounce) packages cream cheese, softened
- 1/2 cup peanut butter
- 1/4 cup white sugar
- 1 egg
- 2 tablespoons milk
- 1 cup butter or margarine, melted
- 2 cups white sugar
- 2 teaspoons vanilla extract
- 3 eggs
- 3/4 cup unsweetened cocoa powder

- 1 1/4 cups all-purpose flour
- 1/2 teaspoon baking powder
- 1/4 teaspoon salt
- 1 cup semisweet chocolate chips

Direction

- Preheat an oven to 175°C/350°F then grease 1 9x13-in. baking pan.
- Beat milk, 1 egg, 1/4 cup white sugar, peanut butter and cream cheese till smooth in medium bowl; put aside.
- Mix vanilla, 2 cups white sugar and melted butter in big bowl; mix leftover, one by one, 3 eggs in, beating well after each. Mix salt, baking powder, cocoa and flour; mix into batter. Mix chocolate chips in.
- Take 1 cup chocolate batter; spread leftover batter in prepped pan. Spread peanut butter filling over; by teaspoonful, drop reserved chocolate batter on filling. Use knife to swirl through top layers gently for a marbled effect.
- In preheated oven, bake for 35-40 minutes till inserted wooden toothpick near middle exits nearly clean. Completely cool; cut to bars.

Nutrition Information

- Calories: 182 calories;
- Total Fat: 10.8
- Sodium: 99
- Total Carbohydrate: 20.7
- Cholesterol: 39
- Protein: 3

62. Milk Duds® Munchies

Serving: 72 | Prep: 25mins | Ready in:

Ingredients

- 2 cups white sugar, divided
- 1 1/2 cups shortening
- 1 1/2 cups peanut butter

- 1 1/2 cups packed brown sugar
- 4 eggs
- 3 3/4 cups all-purpose flour
- 2 teaspoons baking soda
- 1 1/2 teaspoons baking powder
- 1/2 teaspoon salt
- 10 ounces chocolate-covered caramel candies (such as Milk Duds®)

Direction

- Preheat an oven to 175°C/350°F.
- Use electric mixer to beat brown sugar, peanut butter, shortening and 1 1/2 cup white sugar till creamy in big bowl; one by one, beat eggs in.
- Mix salt, baking powder, baking soda and flour in bowl; slowly mix into creamed shortening mixture till dough is combined then chill dough for 2 hours till firm.
- Put leftover white sugar in shallow bowl.
- With a tablespoon, scoop portion of dough; press chocolate-covered caramel in middle. Use dough to cover up; roll to ball then roll dough balls into sugar. Put on ungreased baking sheets.
- In preheated oven, bake for 9-12 minutes till lightly golden and edges are firm. Cool for 5 minutes on baking sheets. Transfer to wire rack; completely cool.

Nutrition Information

- Calories: 154 calories;
- Sodium: 99
- Total Carbohydrate: 18.8
- Cholesterol: 11
- Protein: 2.6
- Total Fat: 8.1

63. Moist And Chewy Peanut Butter Cookies

Serving: 18 | Prep: | Ready in:

Ingredients

- 1/2 cup reduced fat margarine
- 1/2 cup reduced fat peanut butter
- 1/2 cup white sugar
- 3/4 cup packed brown sugar
- 1 egg
- 1 1/4 cups all-purpose flour
- 1/2 teaspoon baking powder
- 3/4 teaspoon baking soda
- 1 pinch salt

Direction

- Mix egg, sugar, peanut butter and margarine; mix flour, salt, baking soda and baking powder in.
- Chill dough for a few hours – overnight.
- Roll dough to 1 1/4-in. balls; put on lightly greased baking sheet, 3-in. apart. Use fork dipped in sugar/flour to flatten crisscross style.
- Bake at 190°C/375°F for 10 minutes.

Nutrition Information

- Calories: 154 calories;
- Cholesterol: 10
- Protein: 3.3
- Total Fat: 5.3
- Sodium: 176
- Total Carbohydrate: 23.7

64. Molasses Peanut Butter Crinkles

Serving: 12 | Prep: | Ready in:

Ingredients

- 1 cup packed brown sugar
- 1/2 cup peanut butter
- 1/4 cup butter, softened
- 1/4 cup molasses
- 1 egg

- 2 cups all-purpose flour
- 2 teaspoons baking soda
- 1/2 teaspoon ground ginger
- 1/2 teaspoon ground cloves
- 1/2 teaspoon salt
- 1/3 cup granulated sugar for decoration

Direction

- Preheat an oven to 190°C/375°F/
- Mix egg, molasses, butter, peanut butter and brown sugar in big bowl.
- Sift salt, cloves, ginger, baking soda and flour in medium bowl; add dry ingredients to wet ingredients. Mix till blended well.
- For every cookie: Form generous dough tablespoon to ball; roll in granulated sugar. Put cookies on ungreased cookie sheet, 2-in. apart. Bake till just set for 10 minutes. Put on wire rack; cool.

Nutrition Information

- Calories: 290 calories;
- Total Carbohydrate: 46.8
- Cholesterol: 26
- Protein: 5.4
- Total Fat: 9.9
- Sodium: 397

65. Mom's Peanut Butter Blossom Cookies

Serving: 48 | Prep: 15mins | Ready in:

Ingredients

- 3/4 cup peanut butter
- 1/2 cup shortening
- 1/3 cup white sugar
- 1/3 cup light brown sugar
- 1 egg
- 2 tablespoons milk
- 1 teaspoon vanilla extract

- 1 1/2 cups all-purpose flour
- 1 teaspoon baking soda
- 1/2 teaspoon salt
- 1 (8 ounce) package milk chocolate candy kisses (such as Hershey's Kisses®), unwrapped

Direction

- Preheat the oven to 375°F (190°C).
- In a bowl, beat together the shortening and butter with an electric mixer until creamy and smooth; add brown sugar and white sugar; beat until fluffy. Add vanilla extract, milk and egg to cream the mixture; beat until mixture is smooth.
- In a separate bowl, mix together the salt, baking soda and flour; beat into the creamed mixture gradually until dough is just mixed. Form into 1-inch balls and transfer onto a baking sheet.
- Bake for 8 to 10 minutes in the preheated oven, until cookies have the lightly brown color. Force one chocolate kiss into the middle of every cookie immediately. Move cookies to a wire rack and allow to cool.

Nutrition Information

- Calories: 94 calories;
- Sodium: 75
- Total Carbohydrate: 9.5
- Cholesterol: 5
- Protein: 1.9
- Total Fat: 5.8

66. Monkey Peanut Butter Bars

Serving: 12 | Prep: 15mins | Ready in:

Ingredients

- 1/2 cup butter
- 1/2 cup white sugar

- 1/2 cup packed brown sugar
- 1/3 cup peanut butter
- 1 egg
- 1/2 teaspoon vanilla extract
- 1/2 teaspoon baking soda
- 1 cup all-purpose flour
- 1 cup rolled oats
- 2 cups semisweet chocolate chips
- 1 cup confectioners' sugar
- 1/4 cup peanut butter
- 3 1/2 tablespoons milk

Direction

- Cream brown sugar, white sugar and butter; blend baking soda, vanilla, egg and 1/3 cup peanut butter in. Add oatmeal and flour; stir well.
- Spread in 13x9-in. greased baking pan; bake for 20 minutes at 175°C/350°F. Remove; sprinkle chocolate chips.
- Put in oven; bake for 8 minutes. Spread to smooth chocolate chips out; cool then mix icing; spread on bars. Refrigerate till set then cut to eat.
- Icing: Mix 3 1/2 tbsp. milk, 1/4 cup peanut butter and 1 cup confectioners' sugar till it gets spreadable consistency.

Nutrition Information

- Calories: 454 calories;
- Total Fat: 23.4
- Sodium: 179
- Total Carbohydrate: 60.2
- Cholesterol: 36
- Protein: 7

67. Mrs. Sigg's Peanut Butter Cookies

Serving: 48 | Prep: | Ready in:

Ingredients

- 1/2 cup butter, softened
- 1/2 cup butter flavored shortening
- 1 cup white sugar
- 1 cup packed brown sugar
- 2 eggs
- 1 cup creamy peanut butter
- 1 teaspoon vanilla extract
- 2 1/2 cups all-purpose flour
- 1 teaspoon baking soda
- 1 teaspoon salt

Direction

- Cream sugars, butter flavored shortening and butter. Add eggs; blend. Add vanilla and peanut butter then add dry ingredients; mix till blended well,
- Measure out dough tbsp.; roll to balls. Put on lightly greased cookie sheets, 3-in. apart. Use fork to make crisscross pattern.
- In preheated 190°C/375°F oven, bake till set yet not hard for 8-10 minutes; don't over bake. Leave for 2 minutes on sheets then remove; cool. Keep in covered container.

Nutrition Information

- Calories: 129 calories;
- Total Fat: 7.1
- Sodium: 117
- Total Carbohydrate: 14.7
- Cholesterol: 13
- Protein: 2.3

68. Muddy Hearts

Serving: 12 | Prep: 20mins | Ready in:

Ingredients

- 1 egg
- 1 cup crunchy peanut butter
- 1 cup white sugar
- 1 (12 ounce) package milk chocolate chips

Direction

- Preheat an oven to 175°C/350°F.
- Line parchment paper on baking sheet.
- Mix sugar, peanut butter and egg in bowl; the dough should be a bit dry, if it seems too wet, add small amounts of sugar.
- Put dough between 2 wax paper sheets; roll to 1/2-in. thick.
- Use heart-shaped cookie cutter to cut dough.
- Put hearts on prepped baking sheet.
- In preheated oven, bake for 7-10 minutes till edges are golden.
- Completely cool on baking sheet.
- At 30-sec intervals, melt chocolate chips in microwave in fully melted; mix between intervals.
- In melted chocolate, dip sides and bottom of each cookie.
- Put cookies on wax paper; dry.

Nutrition Information

- Calories: 348 calories;
- Total Fat: 20.6
- Sodium: 158
- Total Carbohydrate: 38.3
- Cholesterol: 25
- Protein: 7.6

69. No Bake Chocolate Peanut Butter Cookies

Serving: 24 | Prep: 10mins | Ready in:

Ingredients

- 1 3/4 cups white sugar
- 1/2 cup milk
- 1/2 cup margarine (such as Country Crock®)
- 1/4 cup unsweetened cocoa powder
- 3 cups quick-cooking oats
- 1/2 cup creamy peanut butter
- 1 teaspoon vanilla extract

Direction

- Line waxed paper on a baking sheet.
- In a large saucepan, heat cocoa powder, margarine, milk, and sugar to a boil for 1 1/2 minutes. Take off from the heat and blend in vanilla extract, peanut butter, and oats until the dough is evenly combined.
- Drop dough by tablespoonfuls on the lined baking dish and allow to rest about 50 minutes until firm and cool.

Nutrition Information

- Calories: 165 calories;
- Total Fat: 7.3
- Sodium: 71
- Total Carbohydrate: 23.3
- Cholesterol: 1
- Protein: 3.1

70. No Bake Cookies VII

Serving: 24 | Prep: 10mins | Ready in:

Ingredients

- 1 cup creamy peanut butter
- 1 cup marshmallow fluff
- 1 cup semisweet chocolate chips

Direction

- Mix marshmallow fluff and peanut butter in medium bowl; mix chocolate chips in. Roll to 1-in. balls. Serve

Nutrition Information

- Calories: 110 calories;
- Total Carbohydrate: 9.9
- Cholesterol: 0
- Protein: 3
- Total Fat: 7.5

- Sodium: 54

71. No Bake Peanut Butter Cookies I

Serving: 12 | Prep: | Ready in:

Ingredients

- 2 cups white sugar
- 1/2 cup milk
- 1/4 cup butter
- 2 tablespoons unsweetened cocoa powder
- 3 cups quick cooking oats
- 1/2 cup peanut butter
- 1 teaspoon vanilla extract
- 1 cup chopped walnuts (optional)

Direction

- In a saucepan, combine cocoa, butter, milk and sugar; bring mixture to a boil, cooking 1 minute.
- Remove from heat; add the rest of the ingredients. Stir and mix thoroughly.
- Drop mixture by teaspoonfuls on wax paper, allow to stand for 30 minutes or until cool and dry. Keep in well-enclosed container.

Nutrition Information

- Calories: 375 calories;
- Total Fat: 17.3
- Sodium: 82
- Total Carbohydrate: 51.5
- Cholesterol: 11
- Protein: 7.4

72. No Bake Peanut Butter Cookies II

Serving: 48 | Prep: | Ready in:

Ingredients

- 1 cup white sugar
- 1 cup white corn syrup
- 1 teaspoon vanilla extract
- 2 cups peanut butter
- 4 1/2 cups crisp rice cereal

Direction

- Cook corn syrup and white sugar for 1 minute on medium heat; take off heat. Add crispy rice cereal, peanut butter and vanilla.
- By teaspoons, drop onto waxed paper; when done, they will be slightly soft.

Nutrition Information

- Calories: 108 calories;
- Protein: 2.9
- Total Fat: 5.5
- Sodium: 74
- Total Carbohydrate: 13.8
- Cholesterol: 0

73. No Bake Chocolate Peanut Butter Bars

Serving: 60 | Prep: 15mins | Ready in:

Ingredients

- 2 cups peanut butter, divided
- 3/4 cup butter, softened
- 2 cups powdered sugar
- 3 cups graham cracker crumbs
- 1 (12 ounce) package NESTLE® TOLL HOUSE® Semi-Sweet Chocolate Mini Morsels, divided

Direction

- Grease 9x13-in. baking pan.
- In a big mixer bowl, whip butter and 1 1/4 cups of peanut butter till become creamy. Slowly whip in one cup of powdered sugar. Work in the half cup morsels, graham cracker crumbs and leftover powdered sugar using a wooden spoon or your hands. Press equally to the prepped baking pan. Using a spatula to smoothen the top.
- In a medium-sized and heavy-duty saucepan on the lowest possible heat, melt leftover morsels and leftover peanut butter while mixing continuously till smooth in consistency. Spread on top of graham cracker crust in the pan. Let chill in the refrigerator till chocolate becomes firm, for no less than 60 minutes; chop into bars. Keep in the fridge.

Nutrition Information

- Calories: 135 calories;
- Protein: 2.8
- Total Fat: 8.9
- Sodium: 91
- Total Carbohydrate: 12.4
- Cholesterol: 8

74. Oatmeal Peanut Butter Bars

Serving: 32 | Prep: | Ready in:

Ingredients

- 1 cup peanut butter
- 1/2 cup packed brown sugar
- 1/2 cup corn syrup
- 1/3 cup butter
- 2 teaspoons vanilla extract
- 3 1/3 cups rolled oats
- 1/2 cup flaked coconut
- 1/2 cup sunflower seeds
- 1/2 cup raisins

- 1/2 cup semisweet chocolate chips

Direction

- Preheat the oven to 350°F (175°C). Stir together vanilla, syrup, brown sugar, butter or margarine and peanut butter in a large bowl until mixture is smooth.
- Add all remaining ingredients. Stir properly.
- Press the mixture onto 13x9-inch greased pan. Allow to bake for 20 to 25 minutes. Move to a wire rack and allow to cool then cut into bars.

Nutrition Information

- Calories: 148 calories;
- Sodium: 56
- Total Carbohydrate: 18.4
- Cholesterol: 5
- Protein: 3.4
- Total Fat: 7.7

75. Oatmeal Peanut Butter Cookies

Serving: 48 | Prep: 15mins | Ready in:

Ingredients

- 1/2 cup shortening
- 1/2 cup margarine, softened
- 1 cup packed brown sugar
- 3/4 cup white sugar
- 1 cup peanut butter
- 2 eggs
- 1 1/2 cups all-purpose flour
- 2 teaspoons baking soda
- 1 teaspoon salt
- 1 cup quick-cooking oats

Direction

- Preheat the oven to 350°F (175°C).
- Cream together the peanut butter, white sugar, brown sugar, margarine and shortening

in a large bowl until mixture is smooth. Beat in one egg at a time until well combined.
- Mix together the salt, baking soda and flour; stir into the creamed mixture. Stir in oats until just mixed. Drop onto ungreased cookie sheets by teaspoonfuls.
- Bake in the preheated oven for 10 to 15 minutes or until cookies are just light browned. Remember not to over bake. Allow to cool and then keep in an airtight container to store.

Nutrition Information

- Calories: 120 calories;
- Cholesterol: 8
- Protein: 2.3
- Total Fat: 7.1
- Sodium: 152
- Total Carbohydrate: 12.8

76. Oatmeal Peanut Butter Cookies III

Serving: 12 | Prep: 30mins | Ready in:

Ingredients

- 3/4 cup all-purpose flour
- 1/2 teaspoon baking soda
- 1/4 teaspoon baking powder
- 1/2 teaspoon salt
- 1/2 cup butter, softened
- 1/2 cup peanut butter
- 1/2 cup white sugar
- 1/2 cup packed light brown sugar
- 1 egg
- 1 teaspoon vanilla extract
- 1 cup quick cooking oats
- 3 tablespoons butter, softened
- 1 cup confectioners' sugar
- 1/2 cup smooth peanut butter
- 2 1/2 tablespoons heavy whipping cream

Direction

- Cream together the vanilla, brown sugar, white sugar, 1/2 cup peanut 1/2 cup butter or margarine. Add egg; beat properly.
- In a separate bowl, combine salt, baking powder, baking soda and flour. Add to creamed mixture. Stir well. Add to oatmeal and stir.
- Drop onto greased baking sheet by teaspoons, using a fork, press each mound down to shape 1/4-inch thick cookies. Bake at 350°F (175°C) for 10 minutes or until light browned.
- For filling: Cream together the cream, 1/2 cup smooth peanut butter, confectioner's sugar and 3 tablespoon butter or margarine. Spread mixture onto half of the cooled cookies, top with remaining cookies to make sandwiches.

Nutrition Information

- Calories: 397 calories;
- Cholesterol: 48
- Protein: 7.8
- Total Fat: 23.5
- Sodium: 343
- Total Carbohydrate: 42.2

77. Oatmeal Peanut Butter And Chocolate Chip Cookies

Serving: 18 | Prep: | Ready in:

Ingredients

- 3/4 cup butter
- 1/2 cup white sugar
- 1 cup packed brown sugar
- 2 eggs
- 1/3 cup peanut butter
- 1/4 cup water
- 1 teaspoon vanilla extract
- 1 1/2 cups all-purpose flour
- 1/2 teaspoon baking soda

- 2 cups rolled oats
- 1 cup semisweet chocolate chips

Direction

- Preheat an oven to 175°C/350°F.
- Cream white sugar, brown sugar and butter in medium bowl; one by one, beat eggs in. Mix vanilla, water and peanut butter in. Mix baking soda and flour; mix into creamed mixture. Finally, mix chocolate chips and rolled oats in; by teaspoonfuls, drop on unprepped cookie sheet.
- In preheated oven, bake for 8-10 minutes till cookie edges are lightly toasted. Transfer from baking sheet to wire racks; cool.

Nutrition Information

- Calories: 289 calories;
- Sodium: 124
- Total Carbohydrate: 38.5
- Cholesterol: 41
- Protein: 4.6
- Total Fat: 14.1

78. Old Fashioned Peanut Butter Cookies

Serving: 60 | Prep: | Ready in:

Ingredients

- 3 cups all-purpose flour
- 1 teaspoon baking powder
- 1 teaspoon salt
- 1 cup unsalted butter, softened
- 1 cup packed brown sugar
- 1 cup white sugar
- 2 eggs
- 2 cups peanut butter chips
- 1 cup peanut butter
- 2 teaspoons vanilla extract

Direction

- Preheat an oven to 175°C/350°F; line parchment paper on 2 big baking sheets.
- Mix salt, baking powder and flour in medium bowl.
- Use an electric mixer to beat vanilla, peanut butter and butter till blended well in big bowl; beat both sugars in. scrape down bowl sides; mix 1/2 dry ingredients into mixture. One by one, add eggs; beat well after each. Mix leftover ingredients in; mix peanut butter chips in.
- Roll 1 heaping tbsp. full of dough to 1 3/4-in. diameter ball for each cookie; put balls on prepped baking sheets, 2 1/2-in. apart. Flatten dough balls with back of fork; make crosshatch over tops.
- Bake cookies for 15 minutes till dry on top.
- Cool cookies for 5 minutes on baking sheets; use spatula to transfer cookies to cooling racks; fully cool.

Nutrition Information

- Calories: 150 calories;
- Protein: 3.7
- Total Fat: 7.7
- Sodium: 90
- Total Carbohydrate: 16.6
- Cholesterol: 14

79. Onesy Twosy Cookies

Serving: 18 | Prep: | Ready in:

Ingredients

- 1 cup butter flavored shortening
- 1 cup peanut butter
- 1 cup white sugar
- 1 cup packed dark brown sugar
- 2 teaspoons vanilla extract
- 2 eggs
- 2 teaspoons baking soda
- 2 cups all-purpose flour
- 1/2 teaspoon salt
- 1 cup chopped salted peanuts

Direction

- Cream together the vanilla, brown sugar, white sugar, peanut butter and shortening. Blend for 3 minutes. Add in one egg at a time, beat properly after each addition.
- Sift together the salt, flour and baking soda. Add to peanut butter mixture, mix until combined. Stir in chopped nuts. Chill, with cover, for 2 hours.
- Preheat the oven to 350°F (175°C).
- Pinch off 1-inch balls of the dough and arrange on an ungreased baking sheet. Use floured fork tines to press tops. Bake in preheated oven for 10 to 12 minutes or until golden on edges but still soft in the center. Cool on the sheet for 2 minutes then place on the rack to complete the cooling.

Nutrition Information

- Calories: 386 calories;
- Protein: 7.7
- Total Fat: 23.8
- Sodium: 348
- Total Carbohydrate: 38.3
- Cholesterol: 21

80. Pan Peanut Butter Cups

Serving: 18 | Prep: | Ready in:

Ingredients

- 1 cup peanut butter
- 1 (16 ounce) package graham crackers, crushed
- 4 cups confectioners' sugar
- 2 cups butter, melted
- 2 cups semisweet chocolate chips

Direction

- Combine butter, powdered sugar, graham crackers and peanut butter. Press mixture into a 9x13 inch pan.
- Liquify chocolate chips, and spread on top of peanut butter mixture. Allow chocolate to firm (Cut while still soft or layers will fall apart)

Nutrition Information

- Calories: 564 calories;
- Total Fat: 35.8
- Sodium: 364
- Total Carbohydrate: 60.3
- Cholesterol: 54
- Protein: 6.3

81. Paydirt Peanut Butter Cookies

Serving: 18 | Prep: | Ready in:

Ingredients

- 1 cup butter flavored shortening
- 1 cup creamy peanut butter
- 1 cup white sugar
- 1 cup packed brown sugar
- 3 eggs
- 1 1/2 teaspoons vanilla extract
- 2 1/2 cups all-purpose flour
- 1 1/2 teaspoons baking soda
- 1/2 teaspoon salt
- 1/3 cup vegetable oil
- 3 tablespoons water
- 1 (17.5 ounce) package peanut butter cookie mix

Direction

- Preheat oven to 190 degrees C (375 degrees F).
- In a big mixing bowl, mix water, oil and shortening with peanut butter, included peanut butter in the box mix; blend till becoming smooth. Putting in one at a time,

mix in vanilla, eggs, brown sugar and sugar until well combined.

- Mix baking soda, salt and flour together in a smaller-sized bowl. Once those are combined, put the dry mix from boxed cookie mix into the flour mixture and mix using a whisk to break up any lumps.
- Mix the dry mixture a small amount at a time into the wet mixture and stir well. Finishing mixing dough by hands may be needed.
- Roll dough into one and a half to 2-in. balls and add a baking sheet, leaving 2 to 2 1/2 inches between cookies. Make cross-hatching into dough balls with a fork to flatten to 1/2 to 3/4-in. thickness. Bake for roughly 7-10 minutes at 190 degrees C (375 degrees F), till edges begin to turn light brown. Take out of the oven then let it rest for 5 minutes and remove cookies to a wire rack.

Nutrition Information

82. Peanut Brittle Cookies

Serving: 12 | Prep: | Ready in:

Ingredients

- 1/2 cup butter, softened
- 1/2 cup packed brown sugar
- 1 egg
- 1 teaspoon vanilla extract
- 1 cup all-purpose flour
- 1/4 teaspoon baking soda
- 1/2 teaspoon ground cinnamon
- 1 1/2 cups chopped peanuts

Direction

- Preheat an oven to 165°C/325°F then grease 15x9-in. pan.
- Cream sugar and butter in medium bowl; mix vanilla and egg in. Sift cinnamon, baking soda

and flour; mix into creamed mixture. Mix 1 cup peanuts in.

- Evenly spread mixture in prepped baking pan; sprinkle top with leftover peanuts. In preheated oven, bake for 20-25 minutes till edges pull away from pan's sides. Cool; cut to bars.

Nutrition Information

- Calories: 244 calories;
- Protein: 6.1
- Total Fat: 16.4
- Sodium: 90
- Total Carbohydrate: 20.2
- Cholesterol: 36

83. Peanut Butter "Snickerdoodles"

Serving: 24 | Prep: 40mins | Ready in:

Ingredients

- 2 cups butter, softened
- 2 cups peanut butter
- 2 cups white sugar
- 2 cups brown sugar
- 4 eggs
- 4 teaspoons vanilla extract
- 6 cups all-purpose flour
- 2 teaspoons baking soda
- 2 teaspoons baking powder
- 1 teaspoon salt
- 24 fun size bars chocolate-coated caramel-peanut nougat candy
- 1/2 cup white sugar, for sprinkling

Direction

- Preheat oven to 190°C or 375°F. Use parchment paper to line baking sheets then put aside.
- In a large-size bowl, whip brown sugar, 2 cups of white sugar, peanut butter and butter,

whisking till become well mixed and creamy. Whisk in eggs and the vanilla extract.

- Mix salt, baking powder, baking soda, and flour in another bowl. Stir the flour mixture, one cup at a time, to the butter mixture, and mix till you have smooth dough.
- Spoon up a quarter cup dough on each cookie, and shape it into a ball around a fun size candy bar. Place the balls into a baking sheet with no less than 6 in. apart, and using a fork to flatten each ball to a crosshatch pattern, ensure that the cookie dough is still entirely covering the candy bar. Drizzle each cookie using roughly half tsp. of white sugar.
- Bake the cookies for 12-14 minutes till browned the edges a bit in the preheated oven.

Nutrition Information

- Calories: 633 calories;
- Cholesterol: 74
- Protein: 11.3
- Total Fat: 32
- Sodium: 516
- Total Carbohydrate: 79

84. Peanut Butter Balls I

Serving: 48 | Prep: | Ready in:

Ingredients

- 4 tablespoons butter
- 2 cups confectioners' sugar
- 1 cup shredded coconut
- 1 cup chopped walnuts
- 2/3 cup peanut butter
- 1/2 cup maraschino cherries, chopped
- 2 1/4 cups semisweet chocolate chips
- 1 cup flaked coconut

Direction

- Melt margarine/butter on low heat. Take off heat; mix cherries, peanut butter, walnuts, coconut, confectioners' sugar and melted butter. Shape to small balls; chill till firm.
- Melt chocolate chips on low heat. In each ball, stick a toothpick; dip into chocolate then roll chocolate covered peanut butter balls into the coconut to coat. Chill.

Nutrition Information

- Calories: 120 calories;
- Total Fat: 7.6
- Sodium: 33
- Total Carbohydrate: 13.3
- Cholesterol: 3
- Protein: 1.7

85. Peanut Butter Balls II

Serving: 72 | Prep: | Ready in:

Ingredients

- 1 1/2 cups peanut butter
- 1 cup butter
- 4 cups confectioners' sugar
- 1 1/3 cups graham cracker crumbs
- 2 cups semisweet chocolate chips
- 1 tablespoon shortening

Direction

- Mix graham cracker crumbs, confectioners' sugar, margarine/butter and peanut butter; form to 1-in. balls.
- Melt shortening and chocolate chips in top of double boiler; in chocolate mixture, dip balls. Dry on waxed paper. Use toothpick to poke each ball to dip easily.

Nutrition Information

- Calories: 111 calories;

- Protein: 1.7
- Total Fat: 7
- Sodium: 53
- Total Carbohydrate: 11.8
- Cholesterol: 7

86. Peanut Butter Balls III

Serving: 24 | Prep: | Ready in:

Ingredients

- 2 cups creamy peanut butter
- 1/2 cup butter
- 4 cups confectioners' sugar
- 3 cups crisp rice cereal
- 2 cups semisweet chocolate chips

Direction

- Melt butter and peanut butter in saucepan on low heat. Mix confectioners' sugar and crispy rice cereal well in big bowl. Put butter and melted peanut butter on sugar and cereal; thoroughly blend.
- Shape to 1-in./smaller balls then spread on cookie sheets. Chill in the fridge till firm (overnight is okay).
- In double boiler, melt chocolate and keep melted as you work with balls. A teaspoon works best when dipping balls into chocolate; dip well then put on cookie sheet. While dipping them, put them back on cookie sheet then keep chilled till firm.

Nutrition Information

- Calories: 318 calories;
- Total Fat: 18.9
- Sodium: 154
- Total Carbohydrate: 36
- Cholesterol: 10
- Protein: 6.3

87. Peanut Butter Balls IV

Serving: 30 | Prep: | Ready in:

Ingredients

- 1/4 cup butter
- 1 1/2 cups peanut butter
- 4 cups confectioners' sugar
- 1 teaspoon vanilla extract
- 1 teaspoon maple flavored extract
- 2 cups semisweet chocolate chips

Direction

- Cream and knead maple flavoring, vanilla, confectioners' sugar, peanut butter and butter well.
- Melt chocolate chips on low heat; roll dough to 1-in. balls then dip into melted chocolate chips.
- Refrigerate for 15 minutes minimum – overnight on wax paper-lined cookie sheet.

Nutrition Information

- Calories: 206 calories;
- Total Fat: 11.4
- Sodium: 72
- Total Carbohydrate: 25.6
- Cholesterol: 4
- Protein: 3.7

88. Peanut Butter Balls V

Serving: 100 | Prep: | Ready in:

Ingredients

- 1/2 cup butter, softened
- 2 teaspoons vanilla extract
- 1/8 teaspoon salt
- 2 cups creamy peanut butter

- 2 cups confectioners' sugar
- 2 cups chopped pecans
- 2 1/2 cups graham cracker crumbs
- 1 cup confectioners' sugar
- 2 cups semisweet chocolate chips
- 2 tablespoons shortening

Direction

- Cream peanut butter, salt, vanilla and butter together. Mix in all but half cup of the graham cracker crumbs, nuts and 2 cups confectioners' sugar. Put in the last half cup of graham cracker crumbs only if necessary; otherwise it could be hard to mold balls.
- Shape the mixture by hand into 1 in. balls. Roll each ball in the leftover cup of confectioners' sugar. Place the balls in a single layer onto a cookie sheet and let chill in the refrigerator till becoming firm. At this point the cookies could be left plain or dipped into melted chocolate. Keep in an airtight container in fridge to store.
- To Dip Balls into Chocolate: In the top half of a double boiler; melt the shortening and chocolate chips just till the chips are melted. Take out of the heat but leave above hot water. Insert a toothpick into the chilled balls and dip it into the melted chocolate till becoming coated. Place on the waxed paper till becoming hard.

Nutrition Information

- Calories: 95 calories;
- Sodium: 46
- Total Carbohydrate: 8.6
- Cholesterol: 2
- Protein: 1.8
- Total Fat: 6.6

89. Peanut Butter Balls VI

Serving: 18 | Prep: | Ready in:

Ingredients

- 1/2 cup unsalted butter
- 1/2 cup peanut butter
- 1/3 cup white sugar
- 2 teaspoons water
- 2 teaspoons vanilla extract
- 2 cups sifted all-purpose flour
- 1 cup chopped pecans
- 1/2 cup confectioners' sugar

Direction

- Cream together sugar, peanut butter and butter in a medium bowl. Stir in flour and vanilla, then mix well. Mix in pecans. Cover the dough; let it chill 3 hours or overnight.
- Start preheating the oven to 325°F (165°C).
- Roll to form the cookie dough into the walnut sized balls. Arrange on unprepared cookie sheet. Bake in prepared oven for 15-20 mins. Let them cool slightly. Roll in the confectioners' sugar.

Nutrition Information

- Calories: 208 calories;
- Sodium: 34
- Total Carbohydrate: 19.9
- Cholesterol: 14
- Protein: 3.8
- Total Fat: 13.2

90. Peanut Butter Balls VIII

Serving: 40 | Prep: 12mins | Ready in:

Ingredients

- 2 cups peanut butter
- 2 1/2 cups whole bran cereal
- 2 cups powdered milk
- 1 1/2 cups raisins
- 3/4 cup honey

Direction

- Using a wooden spoon or hands to whisk honey, raisins, powdered milk, bran cereal and peanut butter in a big bowl. Roll dough into the walnut-sized balls. Keep chilled in the refrigerator till serving.

Nutrition Information

- Calories: 151 calories;
- Total Fat: 8.3
- Sodium: 97
- Total Carbohydrate: 16.6
- Cholesterol: 6
- Protein: 5.3

91. Peanut Butter Banana Chip Cookies

Serving: 36 | Prep: 20mins | Ready in:

Ingredients

- 1/2 cup butter, at room temperature
- 1/2 cup smooth peanut butter
- 1/2 cup brown sugar
- 1/2 cup white sugar
- 1 egg
- 1 cup all-purpose flour
- 1 cup crushed banana chips
- 1/4 teaspoon salt
- 1/4 teaspoon baking soda
- 1 pinch ground nutmeg

Direction

- Preheat an oven to 175°C/350°F.
- Use electric mixer to beat egg, white sugar, brown sugar, peanut butter and butter till creamy in big bowl.
- Mix nutmeg, baking soda, salt, banana chips and flour in another bowl; blend into creamed

butter mixture. Use flour to dust your hands; roll mixture to 3/4-in. balls.
- Out cookie balls onto ungreased baking sheets; use fork to press down on every ball gently.
- In preheated oven, bake for 10 minutes till lightly browned; on wire rack, cool.

Nutrition Information

- Calories: 100 calories;
- Total Fat: 5.8
- Sodium: 63
- Total Carbohydrate: 11.3
- Cholesterol: 12
- Protein: 1.5

92. Peanut Butter Banana Protein Bars

Serving: 10 | Prep: 15mins | Ready in:

Ingredients

- 2 cups quick cooking oats
- 1 cup protein powder
- 1/4 cup whole wheat flour
- 1 tablespoon ground flax seed
- 1 cup peanut butter
- 1/4 cup honey
- 2 very ripe bananas

Direction

- Preheat an oven to 175°C/350°F. Line parchment on baking sheet.
- On unlined baking sheet, spread oats out to thin layer. Toast for 10 minutes till light brown; remove. Cool. Mix flax seed, whole wheat flour, protein powder and cooled oats till combined well. Mix with honey and peanut butter. Mash bananas into mixture; mix to combine. Press dough down in a 1/2-in. layer on parchment-lined baking sheet.

- In preheated oven, bake for 15 minutes till dough edges are golden brown. Slice to bars while warm. Let bars cool. Use plastic wrap to wrap bars. Refrigerate till serving time.

Nutrition Information

- Calories: 337 calories;
- Cholesterol: 0
- Protein: 22.5
- Total Fat: 15.6
- Sodium: 120
- Total Carbohydrate: 31.7

93. Peanut Butter Bars I

Serving: 12 | Prep: 25mins | Ready in:

Ingredients

- 1 cup butter or margarine, melted
- 2 cups graham cracker crumbs
- 2 cups confectioners' sugar
- 1 cup peanut butter
- 1 1/2 cups semisweet chocolate chips
- 4 tablespoons peanut butter

Direction

- Mix 1 cup peanut butter, confectioners' sugar, graham cracker crumbs and margarine/butter till well blended in medium bowl; evenly press in bottom of 9x13-in. ungreased pan.
- Melt chocolate chips and peanut butter, occasionally mixing till smooth, in metal bowl above simmering water/microwave. Spread on prepped crust; refrigerate for no less than 1 hour. Cut to squares.

Nutrition Information

- Calories: 532 calories;
- Total Carbohydrate: 49.2
- Cholesterol: 41

- Protein: 8.8
- Total Fat: 36.6
- Sodium: 320

94. Peanut Butter Bars III

Serving: 12 | Prep: | Ready in:

Ingredients

- 1 cup shortening
- 1 cup packed brown sugar
- 1 egg
- 1 teaspoon vanilla extract
- 2 cups all-purpose flour
- 1/2 teaspoon salt
- 2 cups confectioners' sugar
- 1/2 cup peanut butter
- 1 tablespoon butter
- 1 teaspoon vanilla extract
- 1/2 cup milk

Direction

- Cream sugar and shortening. Put in 1 tsp. of vanilla and the beaten egg; mix in salt and flour. Stir them well. Spread into the bottom of one 13x9-in. buttered pan.
- Bake for 15 minutes in the preheated oven at 175°C or 350°F. Allow it to cool down.
- For making frosting: Whisk 1 tsp. of vanilla, margarine or butter, peanut butter, and confectioners' sugar. Pour in just enough milk for the right consistency. Frost cooled bars.

Nutrition Information

- Calories: 460 calories;
- Protein: 5.7
- Total Fat: 24.4
- Sodium: 169
- Total Carbohydrate: 56.5
- Cholesterol: 19

95. Peanut Butter Bars IV

Serving: 18 | Prep: | Ready in:

Ingredients

- 1 cup peanut butter
- 6 tablespoons butter
- 3/4 cup packed brown sugar
- 1/2 cup white sugar
- 1 teaspoon vanilla extract
- 3 eggs
- 1 cup all-purpose flour
- 2 cups semisweet chocolate chips

Direction

- Whisk sugars, margarine or butter, and peanut butter together till becoming creamy. Mix in vanilla. Whip in eggs. Stir in flour. Mix in three quarters cup of chocolate chips. Spread dough into the greased 13x9 inch pan.
- Bake for 20-25 minutes at 175 degrees C (350 degrees F). Take pan out of the oven, and drizzle with the remaining of the chocolate chips. Let it rest for 5 minutes and spread. Allow it to cool down, and chop into bars.

Nutrition Information

- Calories: 302 calories;
- Cholesterol: 41
- Protein: 6.2
- Total Fat: 17.6
- Sodium: 110
- Total Carbohydrate: 34.5

96. Peanut Butter Bliss Cookies Vegan, Gluten Free, No Sugar Added

Serving: 24 | Prep: 20mins | Ready in:

Ingredients

- 1 1/4 cups finely chopped pitted dates
- 1 cup natural peanut butter
- 1/4 cup almond milk
- 2 teaspoons vanilla extract
- 1/2 cup oat flour, or more as needed
- 1 teaspoon baking soda
- 1/2 teaspoon salt (optional)
- 2 tablespoons raisins, or to taste

Direction

- Preheat an oven to 190°C/375°F; line parchment paper on 2 baking sheets.
- Process peanut butter and dates in 15-sec intervals on high in food processor; add almond milk slowly while processing till mixture is smooth then add vanilla extract. Stir well.
- Mix salt, baking soda and oat flour in bowl; stir date mixture into flour mixture, if needed add more oat flour till dough holds together. Shape dough, 1-2 tbsp. each, to balls; put on prepped baking sheets. Press fork in every dough ball; dip fork into water after every press; press few raisins gently into each one.
- In preheated oven, bake for 8-12 minutes till edges just begin to be golden; fully cool before eating.

Nutrition Information

- Calories: 104 calories;
- Sodium: 131
- Total Carbohydrate: 11.5
- Cholesterol: 0
- Protein: 3.2
- Total Fat: 5.9

97. Peanut Butter Blossoms

Serving: 48 | Prep: 15mins | Ready in:

Ingredients

- 1 1/2 cups peanut butter
- 1 cup shortening
- 2/3 cup white sugar
- 2/3 cup brown sugar
- 1/4 cup milk
- 2 eggs
- 2 teaspoons vanilla extract
- 3 cups flour
- 2 teaspoons baking soda
- 1 teaspoon salt
- 1/4 cup white sugar, or as needed
- 2 (12 ounce) bags milk chocolate candy kisses (such as Hershey's Kisses®), unwrapped

Direction

- Use electric mixer to beat vanilla extract, eggs, milk, brown sugar, 2/3 cup white sugar, shortening and peanut butter till smooth and creamy in big bowl.
- Sift salt, baking soda and flour in bowl; fold flour mixture slowly into peanut butter mixture to make smooth dough. Use plastic wrap to cover bowl; refrigerate for 1 hour till chilled.
- Preheat an oven to 175°C/350°F.
- Put 1/4 cup white sugar in shallow bow then scoop dough to 1-in. balls and roll balls in sugar. Put on baking sheets, 1 1/2-in. apart.
- In preheated oven, bake cookies for 6 minutes then rotate sheets; bake for 3 minutes. Press chocolate kiss halfway down middle of each cookie; bake for 2-3 minutes till chocolate starts to lose form and melt. Cool on wire racks for no less than 3 hours till chocolate hardens.

Nutrition Information

- Calories: 216 calories;
- Cholesterol: 11
- Protein: 4.1
- Total Fat: 12.9
- Sodium: 154
- Total Carbohydrate: 22.7

98. Peanut Butter Brownies I

Serving: 12 | Prep: | Ready in:

Ingredients

- 1/2 cup peanut butter
- 2 eggs
- 1 teaspoon vanilla extract
- 1 cup packed brown sugar
- 4 tablespoons butter, softened
- 2/3 cup all-purpose flour
- 1 teaspoon baking powder
- 1/4 teaspoon salt
- 1/2 cup salted peanuts, chopped

Direction

- Preheat oven to 150 degrees C (350 degrees F). Grease one 8-in. square baking pan.
- Cream butter and peanut butter together in a big mixing bowl. Put in eggs, vanilla and brown sugar and whip till become light and fluffy. In another bowl, mix salt, baking powder and flour together. Pour into the butter mixture and stir till well blended. Mix in the peanuts.
- Spread batter equally into the pan and bake till toothpick comes out still clean, about 25 - 30 minutes. Allow it to cool on wire rack and chop into 2-inch square pieces.

Nutrition Information

- Calories: 241 calories;
- Total Fat: 13.2
- Sodium: 232
- Total Carbohydrate: 26.9
- Cholesterol: 41
- Protein: 6

99. Peanut Butter Candy Blossoms

Serving: 20 | Prep: 30mins | Ready in:

Ingredients

- 1 cup butter, softened
- 1 cup creamy peanut butter
- 1 cup packed brown sugar
- 1 cup white sugar
- 2 eggs
- 1 teaspoon vanilla extract
- 2 1/2 cups all-purpose flour
- 1 teaspoon baking soda
- 1/2 teaspoon salt
- 20 fun size bars chocolate-coated caramel-peanut nougat candy

Direction

- Beat peanut butter, butter, white sugar, and brown sugar together in a large mixing bowl until no lumps remain. Beat in vanilla and eggs. Mix in salt, baking soda, and flour until incorporated thoroughly. Chill dough, with cover, until no longer sticky, for a minimum of 1 hour.
- Set oven to 350°F (175°C) to preheat. Measure about 1/3 cup of the dough, and wrap around a candy bar. Repeat the steps with the remaining candy bars and dough. Arrange cookies onto ungreased cookie sheets about 3 inches apart.
- Bake cookies in the preheated oven until edges start to turn brown, for 15 minutes. Allow cookies to cool on baking sheets.

Nutrition Information

- Calories: 395 calories;
- Total Fat: 21
- Sodium: 304
- Total Carbohydrate: 47.2
- Cholesterol: 46
- Protein: 7.1

100. Peanut Butter Carrot Cookies

Serving: 48 | Prep: | Ready in:

Ingredients

- 1/2 cup butter
- 1/2 cup packed brown sugar
- 3/4 cup white sugar
- 1/2 cup peanut butter
- 1 egg
- 1/4 cup milk
- 1 cup all-purpose flour
- 1/4 teaspoon salt
- 1/2 teaspoon baking soda
- 2 cups rolled oats
- 1 cup grated carrots
- 1 cup semisweet chocolate chips

Direction

- Preheat an oven to 190°C/375°F.
- Crema peanut butter, white sugar, brown sugar and margarine.
- Add milk and egg. Sift baking soda, salt and flour; mix in. Mix oats in. Add chocolate chips and carrots. By teaspoon, drop onto cookie sheets; bake for 15 minutes.

Nutrition Information

- Calories: 96 calories;
- Total Fat: 4.7
- Sodium: 56
- Total Carbohydrate: 12.7
- Cholesterol: 9
- Protein: 1.8

101. Peanut Butter Chip Cookies II

Serving: 36 | Prep: 10mins | Ready in:

Ingredients

- 1 cup creamy peanut butter
- 1/4 cup shortening
- 1/2 cup white sugar
- 1/2 cup brown sugar
- 1/3 cup water
- 2 cups buttermilk baking mix
- 2 cups semisweet chocolate chips

Direction

- Preheat an oven to 200°C/400°F then grease cookie sheets.
- Cream brown sugar, white sugar, shortening and peanut butter till smooth in medium bowl; mix baking mix and water in. Mix chocolate chips in; roll to walnut-sized balls. Put on prepped cookie sheet, 2-in. apart. Use fork tines to slightly flatten.
- In preheated oven, bake for 8-10 minutes; cool cookies for 5 minutes on baking sheet. Transfer to wire rack; completely cool.

Nutrition Information

- Calories: 145 calories;
- Sodium: 118
- Total Carbohydrate: 16.2
- Cholesterol: 0
- Protein: 2.7
- Total Fat: 8.8

102. Peanut Butter Chip Cookies III

Serving: 42 | Prep: 20mins | Ready in:

Ingredients

- 1/2 cup unsalted butter, softened
- 1 1/2 cups dark brown sugar
- 1/2 cup white sugar
- 1/2 teaspoon salt
- 2/3 cup peanut butter
- 2 eggs
- 1 1/2 teaspoons vanilla extract
- 2 1/2 cups all-purpose flour
- 2 teaspoons baking soda
- 2 cups semisweet chocolate chips
- 2 cups chopped walnuts

Direction

- Preheat an oven to 175°C/350°F then grease cookie sheets.
- Cream peanut butter, salt, white sugar, brown sugar and butter in big bowl; beat vanilla and eggs in. Mix baking soda and flour; mix into batter to make dough. Mix walnuts and chocolate chips in; scoop dough mounds as big as 2 tbsp. onto prepped cookie sheets, no less than 2-in. apart. Roll dough portions to rough spheres between your hand's palms if batter is crumbly; use bottom of glass to flatten cookies down to 1/3.
- In preheated oven, bake for 10-12 minutes till brown and well risen; don't over bake, they firm up a bit while cooling. Cool cookies for 5 minutes on baking sheet. Transfer to wire rack; completely cool.

Nutrition Information

- Calories: 178 calories;
- Total Fat: 10.6
- Sodium: 113
- Total Carbohydrate: 19.8
- Cholesterol: 15
- Protein: 3.3

103. Peanut Butter Choco Chip Cookies

Serving: 18 | Prep: | Ready in:

Ingredients

- 2 cups peanut butter
- 2 cups white sugar
- 4 eggs
- 2 cups semisweet chocolate chips
- 1 cup chopped walnuts

Direction

- Preheat the oven to 350°F (180°C).
- Combine eggs, sugar and peanut butter in a medium bowl. Use a wooden spoon to mix thoroughly until well-blended and smooth. Stir in nuts and chocolate chips.
- Drop rounded tablespoonfuls on ungreased cookie sheets 2 inch apart. Bake for 10 to 12 minutes or until cookies have the light brown color. Leave on cookie sheets to cool for a few minutes then transfer to wire racks, completely cool. Can be stored up to a week in airtight containers.

Nutrition Information

- Calories: 402 calories;
- Cholesterol: 41
- Protein: 10.4
- Total Fat: 25.4
- Sodium: 149
- Total Carbohydrate: 40.6

104. Peanut Butter Chocolate Chip Cookies II

Serving: 18 | Prep: | Ready in:

Ingredients

- 1/2 cup butter
- 6 tablespoons brown sugar
- 6 tablespoons white sugar
- 1 egg
- 1 teaspoon vanilla extract
- 1 cup natural peanut butter
- 1/2 teaspoon baking soda
- 1/2 teaspoon kosher salt
- 3/4 cup all-purpose flour
- 3/4 cup mini semi-sweet chocolate chips

Direction

- Preheat oven to 190°C or 375°F.
- Cream white sugar, brown sugar with margarine or butter. Put in vanilla and egg. Stir them well. Mix in salt, baking soda and peanut butter. Ensure it is well blended. Put in chocolate chips and flour.
- Drop teaspoons of cookie dough then flatten using fork a bit onto the greased cookie sheet. Bake till just appear the brown hint on edges for 5 to 6 minutes. Avoid overcooking. Allow it to cool down on cookie sheet for 5 to 10 minutes. Then add into the cooling rack.

Nutrition Information

- Calories: 225 calories;
- Sodium: 168
- Total Carbohydrate: 20.4
- Cholesterol: 24
- Protein: 4.9
- Total Fat: 15.1

---

105. Peanut Butter Chocolate Chip Cookies III

Serving: 60 | Prep: 15mins | Ready in:

Ingredients

- 1/2 cup unsalted butter, softened
- 3/4 cup peanut butter

- 1/2 cup packed light brown sugar
- 1/2 cup white sugar
- 2 eggs
- 3 tablespoons orange juice
- 1 teaspoon vanilla extract
- 1 1/2 cups all-purpose flour
- 1 teaspoon baking soda
- 1/2 teaspoon baking powder
- 1/4 teaspoon salt
- 1 1/4 cups semisweet chocolate chips

Direction

- Preheat the oven to 350°F (175°C). Oil the cookie sheet.
- Cream together the white sugar, brown sugar, peanut butter and butter in a large bowl. Beat in 1 egg at a time, then stir in vanilla and orange juice. Combine salt, baking powder, baking soda and flour; stir into peanut butter mixture. Lastly, mix in chocolate chips. On the prepared cookie sheet, drop rounded teaspoons of dough. Cookies should be 2 inches apart from each other's.
- Bake in the preheated oven for about 14 minutes or until the center is firm and the edges are golden slightly. Transfer cookies from baking sheet onto wire racks to cool.

Nutrition Information

- Calories: 77 calories;
- Total Fat: 4.4
- Sodium: 52
- Total Carbohydrate: 8.8
- Cholesterol: 10
- Protein: 1.5

---

106. Peanut Butter Chocolate Chip Cookies From Heaven

Serving: 24 | Prep: | Ready in:

Ingredients

- 1 cup butter, softened
- 1 1/2 cups packed brown sugar
- 2 eggs
- 1 cup peanut butter
- 1 teaspoon vanilla extract
- 2 3/4 cups all-purpose flour
- 1/4 cup cornstarch
- 3/4 teaspoon salt
- 1 teaspoon baking soda
- 1/2 teaspoon baking powder
- 1 cup semisweet chocolate chips

Direction

- Preheat an oven to 180°C/350°F.
- Crema brown sugar and butter; beat vanilla, peanut butter and eggs in.
- Add baking powder, baking soda, salt, cornstarch and flour; mix chocolate chips in.
- Use cookie scoop or roll to balls around 1 1/2 tsp; put on ungreased cookie sheets, 2-in. apart. Slightly flatten; they don't flatten a lot while cooking.
- Bake cookies for 10 minutes.

Nutrition Information

- Calories: 281 calories;
- Cholesterol: 36
- Protein: 5.1
- Total Fat: 15.7
- Sodium: 250
- Total Carbohydrate: 32.2

107. Peanut Butter Cocoa No Bake Cookies

Serving: 24 | Prep: | Ready in:

Ingredients

- 2 cups white sugar
- 1/2 cup butter
- 1/2 cup milk

- 1/3 cup unsweetened cocoa powder
- 2/3 cup peanut butter
- 3 cups quick cooking oats
- 1/2 cup chopped peanuts (optional)
- 2 teaspoons vanilla extract

Direction

- Put waxed paper/foil piece on cookie sheet. Mix cocoa, milk, butter and sugar in medium saucepan.
- Cook on medium heat, constantly mixing, till mixture reaches rolling boil.
- Take off heat; cool for a minute.
- Add peanut butter; mix to blend. Add vanilla, peanuts and oats; mix to stir well. By heaping teaspoons, drop mixture quickly onto foil/waxed paper; completely cool. Keep in dry and cool place.

Nutrition Information

- Calories: 203 calories;
- Total Fat: 9.9
- Sodium: 63
- Total Carbohydrate: 26.5
- Cholesterol: 11
- Protein: 4.3

108. Peanut Butter Cookie In A Mug

Serving: 2 | Prep: 10mins | Ready in:

Ingredients

- 1 tablespoon butter
- 1 tablespoon peanut butter
- 1 tablespoon brown sugar
- 1 tablespoon white sugar
- 1 pinch salt
- 1 egg
- 3 tablespoons all-purpose flour

Direction

- In a microwave-safe cup, put peanut butter and butter. For about 30 seconds, microwave the peanut butter and butter until melted. Mix into the butter mixture white and brown sugar and salt. Put in egg and mix in flour. For 2 to 4 minutes, cook in the microwave until cookie is set.

Nutrition Information

- Calories: 227 calories;
- Sodium: 115
- Total Carbohydrate: 23.6
- Cholesterol: 108
- Protein: 6.5
- Total Fat: 12.5

---

109. Peanut Butter Cookies I

Serving: 18 | Prep: 15mins | Ready in:

Ingredients

- 1/2 cup white sugar
- 1/2 cup butter, softened
- 2/3 cup honey
- 2 eggs
- 1 cup creamy peanut butter
- 2 1/4 cups all-purpose flour
- 1/2 teaspoon baking powder

Direction

- Preheat an oven to 175°C/350°F.
- Cream honey, sugar and butter in medium bowl; mix peanut butter and egg in. Mix baking powder and flour; mix into peanut butter mixture. Form dough to 1 1/2-in. balls; put on cookie sheets, 3-in. apart. Dip fork in flour; deeply press across each cookie top in crisscross pattern.

- In preheated oven, bake for 15 minutes till cookies are browned lightly. On wire racks, cool; keep in tightly covered container.

Nutrition Information

- Calories: 254 calories;
- Total Fat: 13
- Sodium: 124
- Total Carbohydrate: 30.7
- Cholesterol: 34
- Protein: 6

---

110. Peanut Butter Cookies II

Serving: 72 | Prep: 15mins | Ready in:

Ingredients

- 1 cup butter, softened
- 1 cup white sugar
- 1 cup packed brown sugar
- 2 eggs
- 1 cup peanut butter
- 2 cups all-purpose flour
- 2 teaspoons baking soda
- 1/4 teaspoon salt
- 1 cup flaked coconut

Direction

- Preheat an oven to 190°C/375°F.
- Cream brown sugar, white sugar and butter till fluffy and light in medium bowl. One by one, beat eggs in; mix peanut butter in. Mix salt, baking soda and flour; blend in to make soft dough. Mix coconut in; by teaspoonfuls, drop dough on ungreased cookie sheet. Use fork tines to flatten each cookie.
- In preheated oven, bake for 12-15 minutes; on wire racks, cool.

Nutrition Information

- Calories: 85 calories;
- Total Fat: 4.8
- Sodium: 83
- Total Carbohydrate: 9.7
- Cholesterol: 12
- Protein: 1.5

111. Peanut Butter Cookies III

Serving: 24 | Prep: | Ready in:

Ingredients

- 2 cups sifted all-purpose flour
- 2 teaspoons baking powder
- 1/2 teaspoon salt
- 2/3 cup peanut butter
- 1 egg
- 1 (14 ounce) can sweetened condensed milk
- 1 teaspoon vanilla extract
- 1/2 cup chopped walnuts (optional)

Direction

- Sift salt, baking powder and flour; put aside. Cream egg and peanut butter. Put the dry ingredients alternately with the canned milk. Mix till well blended.
- Mix in nuts and vanilla. Drop by tablespoonfuls to the baking sheet that is well-greased. Bake for 10 to 12 minutes till browned a bit at 180°C or 350°F. Take out of the baking sheet instantly.

Nutrition Information

- Calories: 152 calories;
- Protein: 4.8
- Total Fat: 6.9
- Sodium: 146
- Total Carbohydrate: 18.7
- Cholesterol: 13

112. Peanut Butter Cookies IV

Serving: 24 | Prep: 20mins | Ready in:

Ingredients

- 1 1/4 cups sifted all-purpose flour
- 3/4 teaspoon baking soda
- 1/4 teaspoon salt
- 1/2 cup butter
- 1/2 cup peanut butter
- 1/2 cup white sugar
- 1/2 cup packed brown sugar
- 1 egg
- 1/2 teaspoon vanilla extract
- 1/2 cup white sugar for decoration

Direction

- Preheat the oven to 190 degrees C (375 degrees F). Sift salt, baking soda and flour together; put aside.
- Cream brown sugar, half cup of white sugar, peanut butter and butter together in a medium-sized bowl till becoming smooth. Whip in egg, and then mix in vanilla. Slowly mix in the sifted ingredients. Form dough into 1 inch balls. Roll in leftover sugar. Put 2 inches apart onto the ungreased cookie sheets. Crisscross using fork tines.
- Bake in the preheated oven for 10 - 12 minutes. Let it cool down a bit then take out of the pan.

Nutrition Information

- Calories: 142 calories;
- Total Fat: 6.8
- Sodium: 120
- Total Carbohydrate: 18.9
- Cholesterol: 18
- Protein: 2.3

113.   Peanut Butter Cookies IX

Serving: 48 | Prep: 10mins | Ready in:

Ingredients

- 1/2 cup butter, softened
- 3/4 cup brown sugar
- 3/4 cup white sugar
- 3/4 cup peanut butter
- 1 egg
- 1 teaspoon vanilla extract
- 3/4 cup all-purpose flour
- 1/4 cup whole wheat flour
- 1 teaspoon baking soda
- 1/2 teaspoon salt
- 1 cup rolled oats
- 1 cup semisweet chocolate chips

Direction

- Preheat the oven to 190 degrees C (375 degrees F).
- Cream peanut butter, white sugar, brown sugar and butter in a big bowl till becoming smooth. Whip in the vanilla and egg. Mix salt, baking soda, wheat flour, and flour together; mix into the peanut butter mixture. Eventually, stir in the chocolate chips and oats. Drop by rounded spoonfuls into the ungreased cookie sheets.
- Bake in the preheated oven till edges become golden, about 8 minutes. Take out of the cookie sheets and allow them to cool down on the wire racks.

Nutrition Information

- Calories: 95 calories;
- Total Fat: 5.2
- Sodium: 85
- Total Carbohydrate: 11.5
- Cholesterol: 9
- Protein: 1.8

114.   Peanut Butter Cookies VI

Serving: 36 | Prep: 15mins | Ready in:

Ingredients

- 1/2 cup margarine
- 1/2 cup peanut butter
- 1 cup white sugar
- 2 eggs
- 1/2 teaspoon vanilla extract
- 1 cup all-purpose flour
- 1 teaspoon baking powder
- 1/4 teaspoon salt

Direction

- Preheat an oven to 175°C/350°F.
- Cream sugar, peanut butter and margarine in medium bowl; one by one, beat eggs in. Mix vanilla in. Mix salt, baking powder and flour; mix into peanut butter mixture. By rounded spoonfuls, drop on unprepared cookie sheet.
- In preheated oven, bake for 8-10 minutes; don't overbake, they should be chewy and soft. Cool cookies for 5 minutes on baking sheet. Transfer to wire rack; completely cool.

Nutrition Information

- Calories: 82 calories;
- Total Fat: 4.7
- Sodium: 84
- Total Carbohydrate: 9
- Cholesterol: 10
- Protein: 1.6

115.   Peanut Butter Cookies VII

Serving: 24 | Prep: 10mins | Ready in:

Ingredients

- 1/2 cup shortening

- 1/2 cup peanut butter
- 1 cup white sugar
- 1/2 teaspoon vanilla
- 1 egg
- 1 1/2 cups all-purpose flour
- 1 teaspoon baking soda
- 1/4 teaspoon salt

Direction

- Preheat an oven to 175°C/350°F then grease cookie sheet.
- Cream peanut butter, sugar and shortening in medium bowl; beat vanilla and egg in. Mix salt, baking soda and flour; mix into creamed mixture till blended well. Roll dough to walnut-sized balls; put cookies on cookie sheets, 2-in. apart. Use fork dipped in sugar water to press down balls.
- In preheated oven, bake for 8-10 minutes; cool cookies for 5 minutes on baking sheet. Transfer to wire rack; completely cool.

Nutrition Information

- Calories: 134 calories;
- Sodium: 80
- Total Carbohydrate: 15.5
- Cholesterol: 11
- Protein: 2.3
- Total Fat: 7.2

116.   Peanut Butter Cookies VIII

Serving: 48 | Prep: 10mins | Ready in:

Ingredients

- 1 cup crunchy peanut butter
- 1/3 cup water
- 2 eggs
- 1 (18.25 ounce) package yellow cake mix

Direction

- Preheat the oven to 190°C or 375°F.
- Mix eggs, water and peanut butter in a big bowl till becomes smooth and well blended. Mix in the cake mix. Blend completely using your hands if needed. Roll into walnut sized balls or drop by spoonfuls 3 inches apart to the ungreased cookie sheets. By a floured fork, punch each cookie down.
- Bake till turns golden brown for 8 - 20 minutes in the preheated oven. Take out of the baking sheets to allow it to cool on the wire racks.

Nutrition Information

- Calories: 81 calories;
- Protein: 2.1
- Total Fat: 4.2
- Sodium: 98
- Total Carbohydrate: 9.5
- Cholesterol: 8

117.   Peanut Butter Cookies X

Serving: 48 | Prep: 10mins | Ready in:

Ingredients

- 3/4 cup peanut butter
- 1/4 cup shortening
- 1 egg
- 1 (14 ounce) can sweetened condensed milk
- 1 teaspoon vanilla extract
- 1 1/2 cups all-purpose flour
- 2 teaspoons baking powder
- 1/2 cup chopped peanuts

Direction

- Preheat an oven to 175°C/350°F.
- Mix egg, shortening and peanut butter till well blended in big bowl; mix vanilla and sweetened condensed milk in. Mix baking powder and flour; mix into peanut butter

mixture to make dough. Mix chopped peanuts in; form dough to 1-in. balls. Put on ungreased cookie sheets, 2-in. apart. Use fork tines to flatten balls.

- In preheated oven, bake for 8-10 minutes till edges are lightly browned. Transfer from cookie sheets onto wire racks; cool.

Nutrition Information

- Calories: 84 calories;
- Total Fat: 4.7
- Sodium: 45
- Total Carbohydrate: 8.6
- Cholesterol: 7
- Protein: 2.6

118.	Peanut Butter Cookies From Pyure

Serving: 16 | Prep: 5mins | Ready in:

Ingredients

- 1 cup natural peanut butter
- 1/2 cup Pyure Organic All Purpose Stevia Blend
- 1 egg, lightly beaten
- 1 teaspoon baking powder
- 1/2 teaspoon Pyure Organic Liquid Stevia Extract, vanilla flavor
- 1 pinch salt

Direction

- Preheat an oven to 350°F. Beat Pyure Organic All-Purpose Stevia Blend and peanut butter till combined well; beat salt, Vanilla Flavor, Pyure Organic Liquid Stevia, baking powder and egg in till combined well. Bring mixture to a ball; use cling wrap to wrap. Refrigerate for 1 1/2 hours till firm enough to handle.
- Roll mixture to 16 even balls; put on parchment paper-lined baking sheets, 2-in.

apart. Press each ball with fork tines, creating cross hatch pattern over each cookie.

- Bake till golden for 10-12 minutes; stand for 5 minutes on baking sheets. Put on rack; fully cool. When baked, cookies will be soft and require time to set up on the rack while cooling.

Nutrition Information

- Calories: 104 calories;
- Total Fat: 8.8
- Sodium: 87
- Total Carbohydrate: 3.8
- Cholesterol: 12
- Protein: 4.5

119.	Peanut Butter Cookies From The Forties

Serving: 48 | Prep: 10mins | Ready in:

Ingredients

- 1/2 cup peanut butter
- 1/2 cup butter, softened
- 1/2 cup brown sugar
- 1 egg
- 1 1/4 cups all-purpose flour
- 3/4 teaspoon baking soda
- 1/2 teaspoon baking powder
- 1/4 teaspoon salt

Direction

- Cream brown sugar, butter, and peanut butter in a medium-sized bowl till become smooth. Whip in salt, baking powder, baking soda, flour and egg; mi into the peanut butter mixture. Cover the dough and let it chill for no less than 60 minutes.
- Preheat the oven to 190 degrees C (375 degrees F). Roll the dough into the walnut sized balls.

Add the cookies 2 inches apart to the cookie sheet.

- Flatten balls using a fork. Bake in the preheated oven for 10 - 12 minutes. Let the cookies cool down on baking sheet for 5 minutes prior to transferring to the wire rack to cool down totally.

Nutrition Information

- Calories: 52 calories;
- Total Fat: 3.4
- Sodium: 63
- Total Carbohydrate: 4.5
- Cholesterol: 9
- Protein: 1.2

---

120. Peanut Butter Cookies With Chocolate Chunks

Serving: 12 | Prep: | Ready in:

Ingredients

- 1 1/2 cups unbleached all-purpose flour
- 1/3 cup rolled oats
- 1 teaspoon baking soda
- 1/4 teaspoon salt
- 1 cup crunchy peanut butter
- 1 cup packed brown sugar
- 1/2 cup unsalted butter
- 1/4 cup honey
- 1 egg
- 1 teaspoon vanilla extract
- 5 (1 ounce) squares semisweet chocolate

Direction

- In medium bowl, mix salt, baking soda, oats and flour.
- Use electric mixer to beat vanilla, egg, honey, butter, brown sugar and peanut butter till blended well in big bowl; in 2 additions, mix

dry ingredients into peanut butter mixture. Mix chopped chocolate in.

- Cover; refrigerate for 30 minutes till dough isn't stick and is firm.
- Preheat an oven to 175°C/350°F then butter 2 heavy big baking sheets.
- Roll 1 heaping dough tablespoonful for every cookie to 1 3/4-in. diameter ball with hands; put cookies onto prepped baking sheets, 2 1/2-in. apart.
- Bake cookies for 12 minutes till starting to brown on top, very soft to touch and puffed; cool cookies for 5 minutes on baking sheets. Use metal spatula to transfer cookies to rack; fully cool. You can make this 2 days ahead, kept at room temperature in airtight container.

Nutrition Information

- Calories: 416 calories;
- Sodium: 271
- Total Carbohydrate: 48.6
- Cholesterol: 36
- Protein: 8.6
- Total Fat: 22.9

---

121. Peanut Butter Cookies With Truvia® Baking Blend

Serving: 15 | Prep: | Ready in:

Ingredients

- 3/4 cup Truvia® Baking Blend
- 1 cup peanut butter
- 3 tablespoons shortening
- 3 tablespoons unsalted butter plus
- 2 teaspoons unsalted butter
- 1 egg
- 1/2 teaspoon vanilla extract
- 2 cups all-purpose flour, sifted
- 3/4 teaspoon baking soda
- 1/2 teaspoon salt

Direction

- Preheat an oven to 375°F.
- Mix vanilla, egg, butter, shortening, peanut butter and Truvia Barking blend at low speed till combined in big bowl.
- Whisk salt, baking soda and flour in 2nd smaller bowl; slowly add to bigger bowl. Mix till combined.
- Form 1 1/4 inch dough balls; on the bottom and the top, flattening slightly.
- Put cookies on parchment lined/ungreased cookie sheet, 3-in. apart.
- Use fork to press each cookie in crisscross pattern.
- Bake till lightly browned for 12-14 minutes.
- Rest on pan for 5 minutes; put cookies onto wire rack to completely cool.

Nutrition Information

122. Peanut Butter Cornflake Crunch Bars

Serving: 12 | Prep: | Ready in:

Ingredients

- 1 cup light corn syrup
- 1 cup white sugar
- 1 cup smooth peanut butter
- 10 cups cornflakes cereal

Direction

- Cook sugar and syrup till mixture boils; constantly mix, don't overcook.
- Take off heat. Add peanut butter; mix till smooth. Put mixture on cornflakes in big bowl; mix till cereal is coated thoroughly.
- Spread in 9x13-in. buttered pan; lightly press down using buttered hands. Cut to squares when cool.

Nutrition Information

- Calories: 353 calories;
- Total Fat: 11
- Sodium: 284
- Total Carbohydrate: 62.2
- Cholesterol: 0
- Protein: 6.9

123. Peanut Butter Crispies I

Serving: 12 | Prep: | Ready in:

Ingredients

- 1 cup honey
- 1 cup white sugar
- 1/2 teaspoon salt
- 3/4 (12 ounce) package cornflakes cereal
- 2 cups creamy peanut butter

Direction

- In a saucepan over medium heat, whisk salt, sugar and honey together, and boil.
- Put in 2 cups of peanut butter and stir till dissolved. Take out of the heat.
- Put in corn flakes and mix well. Spread in 13x9 in. pan while still warm. Allow it cool down then chop into square pieces.

Nutrition Information

- Calories: 480 calories;
- Protein: 12.3
- Total Fat: 21.8
- Sodium: 449
- Total Carbohydrate: 66.9
- Cholesterol: 0

124. Peanut Butter Crispies II

Serving: 12 | Prep: | Ready in:

Ingredients

- 6 cups crisp rice cereal
- 1 cup white sugar
- 1 cup peanut butter
- 1 cup corn syrup
- 1 tablespoon butter

Direction

- Mix corn syrup, peanut butter and sugar in medium saucepan, don't burn, it will ruin the recipe, mixing till melted well. Take pan off heat.
- Mix crisp rice cereal and warm peanut butter mixture.
- Grease 9x13-in. pan well with margarine/butter; spread mixture in pan then cool. Cut to bars when mixture isn't stick to the touch.

Nutrition Information

- Calories: 323 calories;
- Sodium: 213
- Total Carbohydrate: 52.6
- Cholesterol: 3
- Protein: 6.3
- Total Fat: 12

125. Peanut Butter Cup Brownies

Serving: 6 | Prep: | Ready in:

Ingredients

- 1 (19.8 ounce) package brownie mix
- 1/4 cup vegetable oil
- 3 tablespoons water
- 1 egg
- 20 miniature chocolate covered peanut butter cups, unwrapped

Direction

- Preheat the oven to 325°F (165°C). In a large bowl, combine water, egg, oil and brownie mix. Stir 50 strokes with spoon.
- In a cupcake pan, place batter (we recommend cupcake wrappers). When cups are 3/4 full, press an unwrapped miniature peanut butter cup in the middle of each cup, and bake for 30 to 35 minutes, watching closely on the batter to avoid burning. Allow to cool and serve.

Nutrition Information

- Calories: 628 calories;
- Sodium: 374
- Total Carbohydrate: 85.2
- Cholesterol: 33
- Protein: 7.4
- Total Fat: 31.7

126. Peanut Butter Cup Cookies I

Serving: 18 | Prep: | Ready in:

Ingredients

- 3/4 cup peanut butter
- 1/2 cup shortening
- 1/2 cup white sugar
- 1/3 cup packed brown sugar
- 1 egg
- 2 tablespoons milk
- 1 teaspoon vanilla extract
- 1 1/3 cups all-purpose flour
- 1 teaspoon baking soda
- 1/3 cup granulated sugar for decoration
- 30 miniature chocolate covered peanut butter cups, unwrapped

Direction

- Preheat oven to 180 degrees C (350 degrees F).
- Cream the brown sugar, a third cup of sugar, shortening and peanut butter together in a big mixer bowl. Put in vanilla, milk and egg; whip them well.
- Mix baking soda with flour; slowly put into the creamed mixture, mixing well. Form dough into 1 1/2 in. balls; roll the balls in sugar.
- Put onto the ungreased cookie sheet; bake for 10 to 12 minutes. Take out of the oven and add unwrapped peanut butter cup on top of each cookie INSTANTLY, pushing down so that cookie cracks around edges. Let it cool down a bit; take out of the cookie sheet.

Nutrition Information

- Calories: 271 calories;
- Cholesterol: 11
- Protein: 5.4
- Total Fat: 15.5
- Sodium: 166
- Total Carbohydrate: 29.8

---

127. Peanut Butter Cup Cookies II

Serving: 7 | Prep: | Ready in:

Ingredients

- 1/2 cup butter
- 1/2 cup white sugar
- 1/2 cup packed brown sugar
- 1/2 cup peanut butter
- 1 egg
- 1/2 teaspoon vanilla extract
- 1 1/4 cups all-purpose flour
- 2/3 teaspoon baking soda
- 1/4 teaspoon salt

- 15 miniature chocolate covered peanut butter cups, unwrapped

Direction

- Preheat an oven to 350°.
- Cream peanut butter, brown sugar, white sugar and butter in medium bowl; mix vanilla and egg in. Sift salt, baking soda and flour; mix into creamed mixture.
- By tablespoonfuls, drop into muffin tin cups to 1/4 full; bake till lightly browned for 8-10 minutes. Remove from oven; press peanut butter cup immediately into middle of each cookie; completely cool cookies. Remove from pan.

Nutrition Information

- Calories: 518 calories;
- Total Fat: 28.5
- Sodium: 448
- Total Carbohydrate: 59.7
- Cholesterol: 62
- Protein: 9.7

---

128. Peanut Butter Cup Cookies III

Serving: 24 | Prep: 15mins | Ready in:

Ingredients

- 1 3/4 cups all-purpose flour
- 1 teaspoon baking soda
- 1/2 cup white sugar
- 1/2 cup packed brown sugar
- 1/2 cup shortening
- 1/2 cup peanut butter
- 1 egg
- 2 tablespoons milk
- 1 teaspoon vanilla extract
- 24 miniature peanut butter cups

Direction

- Preheat oven to 190 degrees C (375 degrees F). Grease the mini muffin pans. Sift baking soda and flour together. Put aside.
- Cream shortening, brown sugar and white sugar together in a medium-sized bowl. Put in the egg and peanut butter; stir till blended. Mix in the vanilla and milk alternately along with the dry ingredients. Push down rounded tablespoons of dough into the prepped mini muffin cups. Push dough up the sides of the cup, leaving a hole in the center. Push a peanut butter cup into the cup middle; don't press all the way through the dough.
- Bake in the preheated oven for 10 - 12 minutes. Let the cookies cool down totally prior to taking out of the pans.

Nutrition Information

- Calories: 181 calories;
- Cholesterol: 11
- Protein: 3.4
- Total Fat: 9.7
- Sodium: 107
- Total Carbohydrate: 21.1

129.   Peanut Butter Fingers

Serving: 24 | Prep: 15mins | Ready in:

Ingredients

- 1/2 cup butter, softened
- 1/2 cup white sugar
- 1/2 cup packed brown sugar
- 1 egg
- 1/3 cup peanut butter
- 1/2 teaspoon vanilla extract
- 1 cup all-purpose flour
- 1/2 teaspoon baking soda
- 1/4 teaspoon salt
- 1 cup rolled oats

- 1 cup semisweet chocolate chips
- 1/2 cup confectioners' sugar
- 1/4 cup peanut butter
- 3 tablespoons milk

Direction

- Preheat an oven to 165°C/325°F then grease 9x13-in. baking pan.
- Cream brown sugar, white sugar and butter till smooth in big bowl; beat vanilla, 1/3 cup peanut butter and egg in. Mix salt, baking soda and flour; mix into peanut butter mixture. Mix rolled oats in. Evenly spread dough into prepped pan.
- In preheated oven, bake for 20-25 minutes till edges are firm. Take out of oven; in 1 layer, sprinkle chocolate chips over. Stand for 5 minutes; spread to cover. Cool. Mix 1/4 cup peanut butter and confectioners' sugar till smooth in small bowl; 1 tbsp. at a time, mix milk in till you get drizzling consistency. When cool, drizzle on bars; cut to bars.

Nutrition Information

- Calories: 184 calories;
- Total Fat: 9.6
- Sodium: 113
- Total Carbohydrate: 23.3
- Cholesterol: 18
- Protein: 3.2

130.   Peanut Butter Haystacks

Serving: 12 | Prep: | Ready in:

Ingredients

- 1 cup butterscotch chips
- 1/2 cup peanut butter
- 1/2 cup salted peanuts
- 2 cups chow mein noodles

Direction

- In microwave/in top of double boiler, melt peanut butter and butterscotch chips; blend together.
- Gently mix noodles and peanuts into melted peanut butter mixture.
- By forkfuls, drop dough onto waxed paper then cool till set.

Nutrition Information

- Calories: 219 calories;
- Total Fat: 14.8
- Sodium: 147
- Total Carbohydrate: 16.8
- Cholesterol: 0
- Protein: 4.8

---

131. Peanut Butter Heaven

Serving: 16 | Prep: 10mins | Ready in:

Ingredients

- 1 cup butter, softened
- 1 cup white sugar
- 1 cup brown sugar
- 2 eggs
- 3/4 cup peanut butter
- 2 cups rolled oats
- 2 cups all-purpose flour
- 1 teaspoon baking soda
- 2 1/2 cups semisweet chocolate chips
- 1/2 cup peanut butter

Direction

- Preheat the oven to 350°F (175°C). Glaze a 9x13 inch baking pan with grease. Cream brown sugar, white sugar and butter together in a large bowl. Beat in 1 egg at a time, then stir in 3/4 cup peanut butter. Combine baking soda, flour and oats; stir the dry mixture into creamed mixture until well combined. Evenly press the dough into the prepared pan.

- Bake in preheated oven for 15 to 20 minutes until firm. Melt 1/2 cup peanut butter and chocolate chips together over a double boiler or in the microwave, stirring often until mixture is smooth. Spread on top of cooled bars and allow to set up prior to slicing into squares.

Nutrition Information

- Calories: 533 calories;
- Total Fat: 31
- Sodium: 268
- Total Carbohydrate: 60.7
- Cholesterol: 54
- Protein: 10

---

132. Peanut Butter Hemp Cookies

Serving: 36 | Prep: 20mins | Ready in:

Ingredients

- 2 1/2 cups all-purpose flour
- 1/2 cup raisins
- 1/4 cup hemp seed hearts
- 1 teaspoon baking powder
- 1/2 teaspoon baking soda
- 3/4 cup brown sugar
- 3/4 cup white sugar
- 1/2 cup butter, softened
- 1/2 cup applesauce
- 1 cup natural peanut butter
- 2 eggs
- 1 teaspoon vanilla extract

Direction

- Preheat oven to 190 degrees C (375 degrees F).
- In a bowl, stir baking soda, baking powder, hemp seed hearts, raisins and flour together. With an electric mixer, whip applesauce, butter, white sugar and brown sugar together

in a bowl till smooth and creamy; put in peanut butter and whip till smooth in consistency.

- In a bowl, whip vanilla extract and eggs together; mix into peanut butter mixture. Stir flour mixture into peanut butter mixture till forming a smooth dough. Roll dough into small balls and put onto a baking sheet; push down each to flatten using a fork.
- Bake for roughly 9 minutes in the preheated oven till becoming golden brown.

Nutrition Information

- Calories: 144 calories;
- Total Fat: 7.2
- Sodium: 73
- Total Carbohydrate: 17.6
- Cholesterol: 17
- Protein: 3.5

133.   Peanut Butter Honey Balls

Serving: 12 | Prep: | Ready in:

Ingredients

- 1 cup nonfat dry milk powder
- 1/2 cup peanut butter
- 1/2 cup honey
- 1/2 cup graham cracker crumbs
- 1/4 cup finely chopped walnuts

Direction

- Mix graham cracker crumbs, honey, peanut butter and milk powder till blended in small bowl. Form to 1-in. balls; roll into chopped nuts then chill.

Nutrition Information

- Calories: 173 calories;

- Sodium: 125
- Total Carbohydrate: 22
- Cholesterol: 2
- Protein: 7
- Total Fat: 7.4

134.   Peanut Butter Kiss Cookies

Serving: 9 | Prep: | Ready in:

Ingredients

- 1 cup white sugar
- 1 cup peanut butter
- 1 egg
- 18 milk chocolate candy kisses, unwrapped

Direction

- Preheat the oven to 350°F. Combine egg, peanut butter and sugar.
- Form dough into 1-inch balls and put on ungreased cookie sheet (NOTE: if dough is too sticky, chill for 30 minutes until can be easily handled)
- Allow to bake for 10 minutes. Remove from oven. Force 1 chocolate kiss into the center of each warm cookie.

Nutrition Information

- Calories: 311 calories;
- Total Fat: 17.9
- Sodium: 147
- Total Carbohydrate: 33.5
- Cholesterol: 23
- Protein: 8.5

135.   Peanut Butter Kisses II

Serving: 24 | Prep: | Ready in:

Ingredients

- 1 cup creamy peanut butter
- 1 1/4 cups white sugar
- 2 eggs
- 48 milk chocolate candy kisses, unwrapped

Direction

- Preheat an oven to 175°C/350°F.
- Mix eggs, sugar and peanut butter till blended. Roll level dough tbsp. to balls with floured hands.
- 1 1/2-in. apart, put balls; bake for 12-14 minutes. Take out of pan; put chocolate kiss immediately in center then cool for 1-2 minutes.

Nutrition Information

- Calories: 158 calories;
- Sodium: 63
- Total Carbohydrate: 18.1
- Cholesterol: 18
- Protein: 3.9
- Total Fat: 8.7

136.   Peanut Butter Malted Cookies

Serving: 24 | Prep: 20mins | Ready in:

Ingredients

- 1 cup unsalted butter, softened
- 1 cup crunchy peanut butter
- 1 cup barley malt syrup
- 1 cup white sugar
- 2 eggs
- 2 1/2 cups all-purpose flour
- 1 1/2 teaspoons baking soda
- 1 teaspoon baking powder
- 1/2 teaspoon salt

Direction

- In a bowl, beat together the white sugar, barley malt syrup, peanut butter and butter with an electric mixer until mixture is creamy and smooth. Beat in eggs until smooth.
- In a bowl, sift together the salt, baking powder, baking soda and flour; stir into the creamed mixture until just mixed. Chill for 1 hour.
- Preheat the oven to 375°F (190°C).
- Roll dough into 1 inch balls and place on baking sheets. Use a fork to flatten each ball and form a crisscross pattern.
- Bake in the preheated oven for about 10 minutes until cookie edges are browned.

Nutrition Information

- Calories: 268 calories;
- Total Fat: 13.6
- Sodium: 212
- Total Carbohydrate: 32.1
- Cholesterol: 36
- Protein: 5.5

137.   Peanut Butter Mini Candy Coated Chocolates Cookies

Serving: 24 | Prep: | Ready in:

Ingredients

- 3/4 cup butter, softened
- 3/4 cup peanut butter
- 1 1/4 cups packed brown sugar
- 1 egg
- 1 teaspoon vanilla extract
- 1 1/2 cups all-purpose flour

- 1 teaspoon baking soda
- 1/4 teaspoon salt
- 1 3/4 cups mini candy-coated chocolates

Direction

- Cream sugar, peanut butter and margarine/butter till fluffy and light in big bowl; beat vanilla and egg in. Mix salt, baking soda and flour; blend into creamed mixture. Mix 1 1/3 cups mini candy-coated chocolates in.
- Form dough to 1 1/4-in. balls; put on ungreased cookie sheets, 2-in. apart. Flatten gently to 1/2-in. thick. Put 7-8 leftover candies on every cookies; lightly press in.
- Bake for 10-12 minutes at 175°C/350°F till edges are lightly browned; don't overbake. Cool on cookie sheets for 1 minutes. Transfer cookies onto wire racks; completely cool.

Nutrition Information

- Calories: 248 calories;
- Total Fat: 13.3
- Sodium: 170
- Total Carbohydrate: 29.6
- Cholesterol: 25
- Protein: 3.8

---

138.   Peanut Butter Molasses Cookies

Serving: 36 | Prep: 15mins | Ready in:

Ingredients

- 1/4 cup butter, softened
- 1/4 cup peanut butter
- 1/2 cup white sugar
- 1/4 cup honey
- 1/4 cup unsulfured molasses
- 1 egg
- 1 teaspoon vanilla extract

- 1 1/3 cups all-purpose flour
- 1/2 teaspoon baking powder
- 3/4 teaspoon baking soda
- 1/4 teaspoon salt
- 1/4 teaspoon ground nutmeg
- 1 teaspoon ground cinnamon
- 1/4 teaspoon ground ginger
- 1/2 cup white sugar

Direction

- Preheat an oven to 190°C/375°F then grease cookie sheets.
- Cream 1/2 cup white sugar, peanut butter and butter till smooth in medium bowl; mix vanilla, egg, honey and molasses in. Mix ginger, cinnamon, nutmeg, salt, baking soda, baking powder and flour; mix dry ingredients into molasses mixture till blended well. Roll dough to walnut-sized balls; roll balls in leftover 1/2 cup sugar. Put cookies on prepped cookie sheets, 2-in. apart; use fork to press crisscross on top.
- In preheated oven, bake for 8-10 minutes; cool for 5 minutes on baking sheet. Transfer to wire racks; fully cool.

Nutrition Information

- Calories: 77 calories;
- Sodium: 68
- Total Carbohydrate: 13.2
- Cholesterol: 9
- Protein: 1.1
- Total Fat: 2.4

---

139.   Peanut Butter No Bakes

Serving: 18 | Prep: | Ready in:

Ingredients

- 1/2 cup packed brown sugar
- 1/2 cup peanut butter

- 1/4 cup evaporated milk
- 2 1/2 cups crispy rice cereal

Direction

- Boil evaporated milk, peanut butter and brown sugar, constantly mixing, in medium saucepan till peanut butter melts and brown sugar dissolves.
- Take off heat; mix crisp rice cereal in. By rounded teaspoons, drop on foil/waxed paper; cool till firm.

Nutrition Information

- Calories: 84 calories;
- Sodium: 68
- Total Carbohydrate: 11.1
- Cholesterol: 1
- Protein: 2.3
- Total Fat: 3.9

---

140. Peanut Butter Oatmeal Cookies

Serving: 36 | Prep: | Ready in:

Ingredients

- 1 1/2 cups shortening
- 1 1/2 cups peanut butter
- 2 cups packed brown sugar
- 3 eggs
- 2 teaspoons vanilla extract
- 3 cups quick cooking oats
- 2 cups whole wheat flour
- 2 teaspoons baking soda
- 1 teaspoon salt

Direction

- Preheat oven to 180 degrees C (350 degrees F).
- Cream peanut butter, and shortening in a mixing bowl. Put in vanilla, eggs and brown sugar; stir them well.

- Mix salt, baking soda, flour and oats together; put into the creamed mixture and stir them well.
- Drop by the rounded teaspoonfuls into the ungreased baking sheet. Flatten using fork. Bake till done, about 12 minutes.

Nutrition Information

- Calories: 240 calories;
- Total Fat: 14.9
- Sodium: 194
- Total Carbohydrate: 23.6
- Cholesterol: 16
- Protein: 5

---

141. Peanut Butter Oatmeal Cookies II

Serving: 12 | Prep: | Ready in:

Ingredients

- 2 cups white sugar
- 1/2 cup evaporated milk
- 1/4 cup unsweetened cocoa powder
- 1/2 cup butter
- 1/2 cup peanut butter
- 2 cups rolled oats

Direction

- Boil butter, cocoa powder, evaporated milk and sugar while mixing in medium saucepan; Boil for 1 minute, take off heat. Mix rolled oats and peanut butter in; by heaping teaspoonfuls, drop on waxed paper. Cool then serve.

Nutrition Information

- Calories: 329 calories;
- Total Fat: 15
- Sodium: 116
- Total Carbohydrate: 46.6

- Cholesterol: 23
- Protein: 5.6

---

142. Peanut Butter Oatmeal Cookies From Mazola®

Serving: 60 | Prep: 15mins | Ready in:

Ingredients

- 2 1/2 cups all-purpose flour
- 1 cup old-fashioned oats
- 1 teaspoon Argo® Baking Powder
- 1/2 teaspoon baking soda
- 1/2 teaspoon salt
- 1 cup peanut butter, creamy or chunky
- 1/2 cup Mazola® Corn Oil
- 1/2 cup butter or margarine, softened
- 1 cup brown sugar
- 1 cup sugar
- 2 eggs
- 2 teaspoons Spice Islands® Pure Vanilla Extract
- 1 3/4 cups bittersweet or white chocolate chips (optional)

Direction

- Preheat an oven to 350°F. Mix salt, baking soda, baking powder, oats and flour in medium bowl; put aside. Use mixer on medium speed to beat butter and peanut butter till smooth in big bowl; beat oil in. Beat sugar and brown sugar in till blended then vanilla and eggs. Mix chocolate chips (optional) and flour mixture in.
- Form dough to 1-in. balls; put on ungreased cookie sheets, 2-in. apart. Use fork dipped in sugar to flatten creating crisscross pattern. Bake till lightly browned for 10-12 minutes. Transfer to wire rack; fully cool. Keep in tightly covered container.

Nutrition Information

- Calories: 132 calories;
- Total Fat: 7.2
- Sodium: 73
- Total Carbohydrate: 16.1
- Cholesterol: 10
- Protein: 2.3

---

143. Peanut Butter Sandwich Cookies

Serving: 30 | Prep: | Ready in:

Ingredients

- 1 cup peanut butter
- 1 cup butter flavored shortening
- 1 cup white sugar
- 1 cup packed brown sugar
- 1 teaspoon vanilla extract
- 3 eggs
- 3 cups all-purpose flour
- 2 teaspoons baking soda
- 1/4 teaspoon salt
- 1/2 cup creamy peanut butter
- 3 cups confectioners' sugar
- 1 teaspoon vanilla extract
- 5 tablespoons milk

Direction

- Preheat an oven to 190°C/375°F.
- Cream brown and white sugars, 1 cup cream peanut butter and shortening in big mixing bowl; add vanilla. One by one, add eggs; beat well after each. Mix salt, baking soda and flour in small bowl; add to creamed mixture slowly.
- Form to 1-in. balls; put, 2-in. apart, on ungreased cookie sheet. Use fork to flatten balls.
- Bake, depending on size, for 7-8 minutes. I watch carefully and remove them the second they begin to be golden to keep them chewy. On wire racks, cool.

- Filling: Mix vanilla extract, confectioners' sugar, 1/2 cup creamy peanut butter and enough milk to get frosting like and creamy texture in small bowl; spread frosting over 1 cookie then top off to create sandwich.

Nutrition Information

- Calories: 294 calories;
- Total Carbohydrate: 38.1
- Cholesterol: 19
- Protein: 5.2
- Total Fat: 14.3
- Sodium: 173

---

144. Peanut Butter Shortbread Cookies

Serving: 12 | Prep: | Ready in:

Ingredients

- 2 cups natural peanut butter
- 2 cups packed brown sugar
- 2 eggs
- 2 teaspoons vanilla extract

Direction

- Preheat an oven to 350°F.
- In the order given, mix; put on cookie sheet. Press to cookie shape lightly; bake till golden for 10-15 minutes. To half the recipe, you can add chocolate chips.

Nutrition Information

- Calories: 418 calories;
- Cholesterol: 31
- Protein: 12
- Total Fat: 23.4
- Sodium: 135
- Total Carbohydrate: 45.9

---

145. Peanut Butter Spider Cookies

Serving: 48 | Prep: 45mins | Ready in:

Ingredients

- 1/2 cup shortening
- 1/2 cup peanut butter
- 1/2 cup packed brown sugar
- 1/2 cup white sugar
- 1 egg, beaten
- 2 tablespoons milk
- 1 teaspoon vanilla extract
- 1 3/4 cups all-purpose flour
- 1 teaspoon baking soda
- 1/2 teaspoon salt
- 1/4 cup white sugar for rolling
- 24 chocolate candy spheres with smooth chocolate filling (such as Lindt Lindor Truffles), refrigerated until cold
- 48 decorative candy eyeballs
- 1/2 cup prepared chocolate frosting

Direction

- Preheat an oven to 190°C/375°F; line baking parchment on baking sheets.
- Use electric mixer to beat 1/2 cup white sugar, brown sugar, peanut butter and shortening till smooth in big bowl; beat egg into creamy mixture till incorporated fully. Mix vanilla extract and milk into mixture till smooth.
- Mix salt, baking soda and flour in small bowl; add to wet mixture in big bowl. Mix till incorporated fully to a dough. Divide then form dough to 48 balls.
- In wide shallow bow, spread 1/4 cup white sugar; roll dough balls in the sugar to coat. Put on prepped baking sheets, 2-in. apart.
- In preheated oven, bake for 10-12 minutes till golden brown; take out of oven. Press dimple quickly in center of every cookie using wooden spoon's blunt end. Cool cookies for 10

minutes on sheets. Transfer to wire cooling rack; fully cool.

- Cut every chocolate sphere to 2 hemispheres. Rounded side facing upwards, put 1 piece on each cookie.
- Put frosting in pastry bag with small round tip/plastic freezer bag with 1 end cut off. Dap small amount frosting on back of every candy eyeball; stick 2 onto every chocolate candy to make eyes. In 4 thin lines, pipe frosting, beginning at candy base, on every side over cookie to create spider legs.
- Let frosting harden for 30 minutes at room temperature; keep cookies in airtight container.

Nutrition Information

- Calories: 117 calories;
- Total Carbohydrate: 14.4
- Cholesterol: 7
- Protein: 1.7
- Total Fat: 6.3
- Sodium: 78

---

146.   Peanut Butter Thumbprint Cookies II

Serving: 18 | Prep: | Ready in:

Ingredients

- 1/2 cup butter
- 3/4 cup peanut butter
- 3/4 cup white sugar
- 3/4 cup packed brown sugar
- 2 eggs
- 2 tablespoons milk
- 2 1/2 cups all-purpose flour
- 1 cup rolled oats
- 1 teaspoon baking soda
- 1 1/2 cups raisins
- 1/4 cup white sugar
- 3/4 cup water

- 2 tablespoons lemon juice
- 2 tablespoons cornstarch

Direction

- To make cookies, cream peanut butter with margarine. Stir in sugar, and then whip in milk and eggs. Mix in flour, oats and baking soda.
- For making filling: Mix lemon juice, water and raisins together. Heat till almost boiling. Combine cornstarch and sugar; put in enough (cold) water to make a paste. Mix into the raisin mixture and heat till turning clear.
- Form dough into the walnut-sized balls. Place onto the greased cookie sheet. Make an indentation in each ball's middle using thumb, creating a fairly good-sized hollow spot. Use roughly 1 tsp. of filling to fill. Bake for roughly 10 to 12 minutes at 190 degrees C (375 degrees F).

Nutrition Information

- Calories: 315 calories;
- Total Carbohydrate: 49.1
- Cholesterol: 34
- Protein: 6.3
- Total Fat: 11.6
- Sodium: 169

---

147.   Peanut Butter And Amaranth Cookies

Serving: 36 | Prep: 15mins | Ready in:

Ingredients

- 1 1/2 cups water
- 1/2 cup amaranth
- 1 cup peanut butter
- 1 cup white sugar
- 1/2 cup butter, softened
- 1 large egg

- 1 1/2 cups all-purpose flour
- 1 1/2 cups whole wheat pastry flour
- 1 cup quick-cooking oats
- 1 teaspoon baking powder
- 1 teaspoon baking soda
- 1/2 teaspoon salt

Direction

- Boil amaranth and water in saucepan; lower heat to medium low. Simmer for 20 minutes till amaranth grains are fluffy and water is absorbed. Cool it for 10-15 minutes.
- Preheat an oven to 190°C/375°F.
- Beat peanut butter and cooked amaranth till smooth in big bowl; beat sugar in till fully dissolve. Add butter to amaranth mixture; mix. Mix egg in till smooth.
- Whisk salt, baking soda, baking powder, oats, pastry flour and all-purpose flour in bowl; add flour mixture slowly to amaranth mixture, mixing till dough begins to come away from bowl's sides.
- Shape dough to small balls; put on baking sheet, 2-in. apart. Dip fork in flour; use fork to press dough balls to flatten.
- In preheated oven, bake for 15 minutes till set; cool for 3-5 minutes on baking sheet. Transfer to wire rack; fully cool.

Nutrition Information

- Calories: 140 calories;
- Total Fat: 6.7
- Sodium: 135
- Total Carbohydrate: 17.2
- Cholesterol: 12
- Protein: 3.7

148.   Peanut Butter And Bran Cookies

Serving: 84 | Prep: 15mins | Ready in:

Ingredients

- 1 cup butter, melted
- 3/4 cup packed brown sugar
- 3/4 cup white sugar
- 1 teaspoon vanilla extract
- 1 cup peanut butter
- 2 eggs, beaten
- 1 1/4 cups all-purpose flour
- 1 cup wheat bran
- 3/4 cup rolled oats
- 2 teaspoons baking soda

Direction

- Preheat an oven to 175°C/350°F.
- Beat eggs, peanut butter, vanilla, white sugar, brown sugar and butter in bowl. Mix baking soda, oats, bran and flour in another bowl; mix flour mixture into butter mixture till smooth. By rounded teaspoons, drop onto ungreased cookie sheet.
- In preheated oven, bake for 15-18 minutes. Transfer to rack; cool.

Nutrition Information

- Calories: 65 calories;
- Total Fat: 4
- Sodium: 62
- Total Carbohydrate: 6.7
- Cholesterol: 10
- Protein: 1.3

149.   Peanut Butter And Jelly Cookies

Serving: 54 | Prep: | Ready in:

Ingredients

- 1/2 cup shortening
- 1/2 cup peanut butter
- 1/2 cup white sugar

- 1/2 cup packed brown sugar
- 1 egg
- 1 1/4 cups all-purpose flour
- 3/4 teaspoon baking soda
- 1/2 teaspoon baking powder
- 1/4 teaspoon salt
- 1/2 cup any flavor fruit jam

Direction

- Cream sugars and shortening peanut butter in one mixing bowl. Whip in egg. Mix the dry ingredients; slowly put into creamed mixture.
- Keep it covered and let chill for 60 minutes.
- Roll into 1 in. balls; add 2 inches apart onto the greased baking sheets. Flatten a bit. Bake for 10 minutes at 190 degrees C (375 degrees F). Allow to cool on the wire rack. Spread jam on the bottom of half of the cookie; Add leftover cookie half on top.

Nutrition Information

- Calories: 66 calories;
- Sodium: 47
- Total Carbohydrate: 8.6
- Cholesterol: 3
- Protein: 1
- Total Fat: 3.2

150. Peanut Butter And Oat Brownies

Serving: 16 | Prep: 15mins | Ready in:

Ingredients

- 3/4 cup butter, softened
- 3/4 cup peanut butter
- 3/4 cup white sugar
- 3/4 cup brown sugar
- 1 1/2 cups all-purpose flour
- 1 1/2 cups rolled oats
- 1 1/2 teaspoons vanilla extract

- 2 eggs
- 2 teaspoons salt
- 1/2 cup peanut butter, or as needed

Direction

- Preheat an oven to 165°C/325°F then grease jellyroll pan.
- Beat brown sugar, white sugar, 3/4 cup peanut butter and butter till creamy in big bowl. Add salt, eggs, vanilla extract, oats and flour; mix till just mixed. Spread batter in prepped jellyroll pan.
- In preheated oven, bake for 20 minutes till lightly browned; cool brownies for 10-15 minutes in pan. Spread 1/2 cup peanut butter over brownies.

Nutrition Information

- Calories: 338 calories;
- Total Fat: 20
- Sodium: 456
- Total Carbohydrate: 34.2
- Cholesterol: 46
- Protein: 8.2

151. Peanut Butter/Chocolate Chip Cookie Bars

Serving: 20 | Prep: | Ready in:

Ingredients

- 1/2 cup butter
- 1 1/2 cups graham cracker crumbs
- 1 (14 ounce) can sweetened condensed milk
- 2 cups semisweet chocolate chips
- 1 cup peanut butter chips

Direction

- Preheat oven to 350°F.
- Melt butter over low heat.

- Add butter to 9x13 in. pan. Drizzle graham cracker crumbs on top of the butter.
- Add condensed milk on top of crumbs. Drizzle peanut butter and chocolate chips on milk mixture and push down firmly.
- Bake for 25 - 30 minutes.

Nutrition Information

- Calories: 279 calories;
- Cholesterol: 19
- Protein: 5.3
- Total Fat: 15.4
- Sodium: 127
- Total Carbohydrate: 32.1

---

152.   Peanut Surprise Cookies

Serving: 42 | Prep: 10mins | Ready in:

Ingredients

- 1/2 cup margarine, softened
- 1/2 cup peanut butter
- 1/2 cup white sugar
- 1/2 cup light brown sugar
- 1 egg
- 1 1/4 cups all-purpose flour
- 1/2 teaspoon baking powder
- 2/3 teaspoon baking soda
- 1/4 teaspoon salt
- 1 (8.75 ounce) bag chocolate covered creamy caramel candies
- 1/4 cup white sugar for decoration

Direction

- Cream brown sugar, half cup of white sugar, peanut butter, and margarine together in a big bowl till becoming smooth. Whip in the egg. Mix salt, baking soda, baking powder, and flour together; mix into the peanut butter mixture. Keep the dough covered and let chill for roughly half an hour till firm.

- Preheat the oven to 190 degrees C (375 degrees F). Roll chilled dough into 1 in. balls. Push a caramel candy into each ball's middle in order to cover the candy entirely with the dough. Roll balls in leftover sugar and put 2 in. apart on the ungreased cookie sheets.
- Bake in the preheated oven till becomes set, about 10 - 12 minutes. Allow to cool down on the baking sheets for 2 minutes prior to transferring to the wire racks to let it cool down totally.

Nutrition Information

- Calories: 99 calories;
- Sodium: 91
- Total Carbohydrate: 13.1
- Cholesterol: 4
- Protein: 1.5
- Total Fat: 4.8

---

153.   Peanut Ginger Double Deckers

Serving: 12 | Prep: 25mins | Ready in:

Ingredients

- Peanut Butter Dough:
- 1/4 cup unsalted butter, room temperature
- 1/4 cup white sugar
- 1/4 cup packed dark brown sugar
- 1/4 cup creamy peanut butter
- 1/4 teaspoon baking powder
- 1/4 teaspoon baking soda
- 1/4 teaspoon kosher salt
- 1 egg yolk
- 1/2 cup all-purpose flour
- 2 tablespoons all-purpose flour
- Ginger-Molasses Dough:
- 1 cup white sugar
- 3/4 cup unsalted butter, at room temperature
- 1 tablespoon ground ginger

- 1 teaspoon baking soda
- 3/4 teaspoon ground cinnamon
- 1/2 teaspoon ground cloves
- 1/4 teaspoon kosher salt
- 1 egg
- 1/4 cup blackstrap molasses
- 2 1/2 cups flour
- 2 tablespoons chopped crystallized ginger
- 1/4 cup turbinado sugar

Direction

- Heat oven to 350°F (175°C). Prepare the baking sheet by lining using a parchment paper or silicone baking mat.
- For the dough of peanut butter: Mix the brown sugar, butter, and white sugar into a mixing bowl. Using the mixer, beat until equal in color and butter sticks onto the bowl's sides for 3 minutes. Beat in the baking soda, salt, peanut butter, and baking powder until blended. Rub down the bowl sides. Stir in the egg yolks until combined. Pour the flour and beat on low until mixture forms a dough. Use plastic wrap to cover.
- For the dough of Ginger-Molasses: Mix the butter, cinnamon, salt, ginger, baking soda, cloves, and white sugar into a mixing bowl. Whisk the mixture until equal in color and butter sticks into the bowl sides. Rub down the bowl sides and whisk in the egg until blended. Stir in the molasses until combined. Stir in the flour until blended. Add in the crystallized ginger until combined. Rub down the bowl in between each addition.
- Roll out a 1 1/2 teaspoon of the ginger-molasses dough in a turbinado sugar into a ball with a size of a walnut. Place into the lined baking sheet. Use your palm to slightly flatten the ball. Paint the top using water. Roll out a 2 teaspoon of the peanut butter dough in a turbinado sugar into a marble-sized ball, setting over the disk and using a fork for flattening of the dough and creating a crisscross pattern.
- Do again for the rest of the dough. For 10-12 minutes, bake until top edges of cookies turn just golden brown. For 10 minutes, allow cooling onto sheets before transferring into the wire racks to complete cooling.

Nutrition Information

- Calories: 419 calories;
- Total Fat: 19.2
- Sodium: 260
- Total Carbohydrate: 57.7
- Cholesterol: 73
- Protein: 5.7

---

154. Peanutbutteriest Cookies Ever

Serving: 60 | Prep: 15mins | Ready in:

Ingredients

- 1 1/2 cups peanut butter
- 1 cup butter, softened
- 2 cups white sugar
- 1 teaspoon boiling water
- 1/2 teaspoon vanilla extract
- 1 3/4 cups all-purpose flour
- 1 teaspoon salt

Direction

- Preheat oven to 175 degrees C (350 degrees F).
- Cream white sugar, butter and peanut butter in a big bowl till becoming smooth. Mix in the vanilla and water. Mix the salt and flour together; mix into the peanut butter mixture. Drop by rounded spoonfuls into the ungreased cookie sheet. Push down a bit with the tines of a fork.
- Bake in the preheated oven for 10 - 15 minutes. Allow cookies to cool down totally prior to taking out of baking sheets.

Nutrition Information

- Calories: 104 calories;
- Total Carbohydrate: 10.7
- Cholesterol: 8
- Protein: 2
- Total Fat: 6.4
- Sodium: 90

- Calories: 446 calories;
- Total Carbohydrate: 49.1
- Cholesterol: 48
- Protein: 9.9
- Total Fat: 24.2
- Sodium: 277

155. Peanuttiest Peanut Butter Cookies

Serving: 18 | Prep: | Ready in:

Ingredients

- 1 1/2 cups packed brown sugar
- 1 cup confectioners' sugar
- 1 cup peanut butter
- 1 cup butter, softened
- 1 1/2 cups all-purpose flour
- 1 cup rolled oats
- 2 eggs
- 1 teaspoon baking powder
- 1/2 teaspoon salt
- 1 tablespoon vanilla extract
- 1/4 cup real maple syrup
- 1 cup peanut butter chips
- 1/2 cup crushed peanuts

Direction

- Use electric mixer to mix eggs, syrup, vanilla extract, butter and peanut butter.
- Mix baking powder, salt, oats, flour and sugars in another bowl; fold dry mixture into earlier wet mixture when dry ingredients are mixed.
- Add peanut butter chips and crushed peanuts to dough.
- Roll dough to balls; use fork to slightly press. Bake for 12-15 minutes at 175°C/350°F till cookies are slightly browned.

Nutrition Information

156. Perfect Gluten Free Peanut Butter Cookies

Serving: 24 | Prep: 10mins | Ready in:

Ingredients

- 1/2 cup gluten free, casein free margarine
- 1/2 cup brown sugar
- 1/2 cup white sugar
- 1 egg
- 1/2 cup salted natural peanut butter
- 1/2 teaspoon baking soda
- 1 cup soy flour
- 1/4 cup tapioca flour
- 1/4 cup potato flour

Direction

- Preheat the oven to 190 degrees C (375 degrees F).
- Cream white sugar, brown sugar, and margarine in a medium-sized bowl till becoming smooth. Stir in the peanut butter and egg. Mix potato flour, tapioca flour, soy flour and baking soda together; mix into the batter to shape dough. Roll teaspoonfuls of dough into balls and put them 2 inches apart on the ungreased baking sheets.
- Bake in the preheated oven for 8 - 10 minutes. Let cookies cool down on baking sheet for 5 minutes prior to transferring to the wire rack to let cool down totally.

Nutrition Information

- Calories: 122 calories;

78

- Protein: 3.5
- Total Fat: 7
- Sodium: 90
- Total Carbohydrate: 12.4
- Cholesterol: 8

157. Quick Peanut Butter Cookies

Serving: 36 | Prep: 15mins | Ready in:

Ingredients

- 1 cup peanut butter
- 1 cup white sugar
- 1 egg
- 1 teaspoon baking soda

Direction

- Preheat oven to 165 degrees C or 325 degrees F.
- Whisk baking soda, egg, sugar, and peanut butter in a medium-sized bowl till well blended. Roll dough into 1 in. balls, and add onto the ungreased cookie sheets.
- Bake in the preheated oven for 6 to 8 minutes. Let it cool down on cookie sheets till set, prior to removing to wire racks to let it cool down totally.

Nutrition Information

- Calories: 66 calories;
- Protein: 2
- Total Fat: 3.7
- Sodium: 70
- Total Carbohydrate: 7
- Cholesterol: 5

158. Raisin Peanut Butter Bran Cookies

Serving: 24 | Prep: | Ready in:

Ingredients

- 1 cup whole wheat flour
- 1 teaspoon baking soda
- 1/2 cup peanut butter
- 1 cup butter
- 1 1/4 cups packed brown sugar
- 3/4 cup whole bran cereal
- 2 eggs
- 1 teaspoon vanilla extract
- 2 1/2 cups raisins
- 2 cups rolled oats

Direction

- Preheat oven to 175°C or 350°F. Use baking parchment or aluminum foil to line the cookie sheets.
- On medium heat, melt butter in a big saucepan. Put in sugar and peanut butter and mix till becomes melted. Take out of the heat.
- Add into a big mixing bowl and mix in bran cereal. Mix in well vanilla and eggs. Fold in oatmeal and raisins and mix till blended well.
- Sift baking soda and flour then put into the mixture. Stir completely.
- Drop dough by tablespoonfuls to the cookie sheets. Dip a fork into water and press it to flatten the dough to half an in. thickness.
- Bake till lightly colored the cookies for 15 minutes. Reverse the sheet one time while baking. Allow it to cool down on wire racks.

Nutrition Information

- Calories: 240 calories;
- Total Carbohydrate: 33.2
- Cholesterol: 36
- Protein: 4.1
- Total Fat: 11.4
- Sodium: 150

159.   Robin's Peanut Butter Cookies

Serving: 60 | Prep: 10mins | Ready in:

Ingredients

- 1/2 cup butter, softened
- 1/2 cup white sugar
- 1/2 cup brown sugar
- 1 egg
- 1/2 teaspoon vanilla extract
- 1/2 cup peanut butter
- 1 1/4 cups all-purpose flour
- 3/4 teaspoon baking soda
- 1/4 teaspoon salt
- 1/2 cup chopped dry roasted peanuts

Direction

- Start preheating the oven to 375°F (190°C).
- Cream brown sugar, white sugar and butter together in a large bowl until fluffy and light. Beat in egg and stir in peanut butter and vanilla. Combine salt, baking soda and flour; mix into peanut butter mixture. Lastly, fold in chopped peanuts. Roll to form the dough into the walnut sized balls, arrange onto the unprepared cookie sheet, slightly press down using a fork.
- Bake in prepared oven, about 8-10 mins. Let the cookies cool for 5 mins on baking sheet. Then move to cool completely on a wire rack.

Nutrition Information

- Calories: 55 calories;
- Sodium: 58
- Total Carbohydrate: 5.5
- Cholesterol: 7
- Protein: 1.2
- Total Fat: 3.3

160.   Salted Peanut Rolls

Serving: 15 | Prep: 15mins | Ready in:

Ingredients

- 24 ounces salted peanuts
- 2 cups peanut butter chips
- 1 (7 ounce) jar marshmallow creme
- 1 (14 ounce) can sweetened condensed milk

Direction

- Spread 3 cups chopped peanuts on bottom of 9x13-in. glass pan. Melt peanut butter chips in saucepan on low heat/microwave. Take off heat; mix condensed milk and marshmallow cream in. Put on peanut layers; sprinkle leftover 1 cup peanuts over. Chill till set; cut to bars.

Nutrition Information

- Calories: 573 calories;
- Total Fat: 33.9
- Sodium: 492
- Total Carbohydrate: 50.2
- Cholesterol: 9
- Protein: 19.7

161.   Soft Peanut Butter Cookies

Serving: 12 | Prep: | Ready in:

Ingredients

- 1/2 cup margarine, softened
- 1/2 cup peanut butter
- 1/2 cup white sugar
- 1/2 cup packed brown sugar
- 1 egg
- 1/2 teaspoon vanilla extract
- 3/4 teaspoon baking soda
- 1/4 teaspoon salt

- 1 3/4 cups all-purpose flour

Direction

- Combine vanilla, egg, sugars, peanut butter and margarine. Blend very well together.
- Put in salt, baking soda and flour with mixer. Let the dough chill in the refrigerator for 15 mins. Using hand to roll into balls.
- Place on the sprayed cookie sheet. Bake for 7-10 mins in a preheated 350°F (175°C) oven until the edges are very lightly brown. Do not overcook. Keep in plastic storage containers, they will stay soft!

Nutrition Information

- Calories: 270 calories;
- Sodium: 273
- Total Carbohydrate: 33.5
- Cholesterol: 16
- Protein: 5.2
- Total Fat: 13.5

---

162.   Soft And Chewy Peanut Butter Cookies

Serving: 18 | Prep: | Ready in:

Ingredients

- 2 cups all-purpose flour
- 1/2 teaspoon baking soda
- 1/4 teaspoon salt
- 1 1/4 cups packed brown sugar
- 1 1/4 cups white sugar
- 1 cup butter, softened
- 3 eggs
- 1 cup creamy peanut butter
- 2 teaspoons vanilla extract

Direction

- Preheat an oven to 150°C/300°F.

- Use wire whisk to mix salt, soda and flour well in medium bowl; put aside.
- Use electric mixer to blend sugars at medium speed in big bowl. Add butter; mix to make grainy paste, scraping bowl sides. Add vanilla, peanut butter and eggs; mix on medium speed till fluffy and light.
- By rounded spoonfuls, drop on ungreased cookie sheet. Gently press cookies with wet fork in crisscrossed pattern; bake till slightly brown along edges for 18-22 minutes.

Nutrition Information

- Calories: 350 calories;
- Total Fat: 18.4
- Sodium: 222
- Total Carbohydrate: 42.4
- Cholesterol: 58
- Protein: 6.2

---

163.   Stef's Whoopie Pies With Peanut Butter Frosting

Serving: 6 | Prep: | Ready in:

Ingredients

- 2 cups all-purpose flour
- 1/2 cup unsweetened cocoa powder
- 1/2 cup hot water
- 1 teaspoon vanilla extract
- 1 teaspoon baking soda
- 1 cup white sugar
- 1 cup butter
- 1 egg
- 1 tablespoon butter
- 1 3/4 cups confectioners' sugar
- 1/4 cup peanut butter
- 1/2 cup milk

Direction

- Cream 1 cup margarine/butter and egg. Add hot water, vanilla and 1 cup white sugar; mix baking soda, cocoa and flour in well.
- From teaspoon, drop onto cookie sheets; bake for 10-12 minutes at 190°C/375°F. Use Peanut Butter Frosting to sandwich cookies together.
- Peanut Butter Frosting: Blend peanut butter and 1 tbsp. butter; mix confectioners' sugar and enough milk in to create frosting that's soft enough to spread; spread it between flat sides of 2 cookies then sandwich together.

Nutrition Information

- Calories: 811 calories;
- Protein: 10.5
- Total Fat: 40.9
- Sodium: 513
- Total Carbohydrate: 107.1
- Cholesterol: 119

164. Sugar Free Peanut Butter Balls

Serving: 27 | Prep: | Ready in:

Ingredients

- 1 cup margarine
- 2 tablespoons granulated artificial sweetener
- 1 teaspoon vanilla extract
- 2 tablespoons water
- 2 cups all-purpose flour
- 1 egg white
- 1/2 cup chopped peanuts

Direction

- Preheat an oven to 175°C/350°F.
- Beat sugar and margarine till fluffy. Add flour, water and vanilla; stir well. Refrigerate for 1 hour.
- Shape to 1-in. balls then dip into beaten egg white; roll in peanuts. Put onto ungreased

cookie sheets then bake for 10-12 minutes. Keep in airtight container.

Nutrition Information

- Calories: 114 calories;
- Sodium: 81
- Total Carbohydrate: 7.8
- Cholesterol: 0
- Protein: 2.8
- Total Fat: 8.1

165. Sugar Free Peanut Butter Cookies

Serving: 24 | Prep: 10mins | Ready in:

Ingredients

- 2 cups smooth natural peanut butter
- 2 cups granular no-calorie sucralose sweetener (e.g., Splenda ®)
- 2 large eggs

Direction

- Preheat an oven to 175°C/350°F the grease baking sheet lightly.
- Mix eggs, sucralose and peanut butter thoroughly in bowl; by spoonfuls, drop mixture on prepped baking sheet.
- In preheated oven, bake for 8 minutes till center looks dry.

Nutrition Information

- Calories: 138 calories;
- Total Carbohydrate: 4.9
- Cholesterol: 16
- Protein: 6
- Total Fat: 11.7
- Sodium: 62

166.   Super Dooper Peanut Butter

Serving: 48 | Prep: | Ready in:

Ingredients

- 2 tablespoons peanut butter
- 1 cup white sugar
- 3/4 cup packed brown sugar
- 1 cup butter
- 2 cups all-purpose flour
- 1/4 cup unsweetened cocoa powder
- 1 tablespoon baking soda
- 3 tablespoons vanilla extract
- 2 eggs (optional)
- 1 cup semisweet chocolate chips

Direction

- Preheat oven to 190 degrees C (375 degrees F).
- Combine eggs (optional), vanilla, butter, and peanut butter in a big bowl. Whisk together baking soda, cocoa, flour, brown sugar and sugar in a separate bowl.
- Add the dry ingredients to the big bowl and stir together. Fold the chocolate chips into the batter.
- Drop by teaspoon into the baking sheets. Bake for 10 minutes. Serve.

Nutrition Information

- Calories: 109 calories;
- Protein: 1.2
- Total Fat: 5.5
- Sodium: 108
- Total Carbohydrate: 14.2
- Cholesterol: 18

167.   T. T.'s Cookies

Serving: 12 | Prep: | Ready in:

Ingredients

- 2 cups all-purpose flour
- 1 teaspoon baking soda
- 1 teaspoon salt
- 1 cup unsalted butter
- 1 1/2 cups white sugar
- 1/3 cup peanut butter
- 1 egg
- 1 teaspoon vanilla extract
- 2 cups semisweet chocolate chips
- 4 chocolate covered peanut butter cups, chopped

Direction

- Preheat an oven to 175°C/350°F.
- Sift salt, baking soda and flour; put aside. Cream butter and sugar in medium bowl; mix vanilla, egg and peanut butter in. Add dry ingredients; stir well. Fold chopped peanut butter cups and chocolate chips in; form to 2-in. balls. Put, 3-in. apart, on unprepped cookie sheets.
- In preheated oven, bake for 12-15 minutes. Transfer from sheets to wire racks; cool.

Nutrition Information

- Calories: 521 calories;
- Total Fat: 29.7
- Sodium: 361
- Total Carbohydrate: 63.2
- Cholesterol: 57
- Protein: 6.4

168.   The Whole Jar Of Peanut Butter Cookies

Serving: 30 | Prep: | Ready in:

Ingredients

- 1 cup butter, softened
- 1 cup white sugar
- 1 cup packed brown sugar
- 2 eggs
- 1 egg yolk
- 2 teaspoons vanilla extract
- 1 (18 ounce) jar peanut butter
- 2 cups all-purpose flour
- 1 teaspoon baking soda
- 1/2 teaspoon salt
- 1 cup chopped peanuts

Direction

- Cream brown sugar, white sugar and butter till smooth in big bowl. Add vanilla, yolks and eggs; mix till fluffy. Mix peanut butter in. Sift salt, baking soda and flour; mix into peanut butter mixture. Finally, mix peanuts in; refrigerate dough for 2 hours minimum.
- Preheat an oven to 175°C/350°F then grease cookie sheet lightly.
- Roll dough to walnut-size balls; put on prepped cookie sheet. Use fork to slightly flatten; in preheated oven, bake for 12-15 minutes till dry on top. Cool on cookie sheet for a few minutes. Transfer to rack; fully cool. Cookies are best when slightly undercooked.

Nutrition Information

- Calories: 272 calories;
- Cholesterol: 35
- Protein: 6.9
- Total Fat: 17.5
- Sodium: 210
- Total Carbohydrate: 24.5

---

169.   Three Ingredient Peanut Butter Cookies

Serving: 6 | Prep: | Ready in:

Ingredients

- 1 cup peanut butter
- 1 cup white sugar
- 1 egg

Direction

- Preheat an oven to 175°C/350°F; line parchment paper on baking sheets.
- Mix egg, white sugar and peanut butter till smooth.
- Drop dough spoonfuls on prepped baking sheet; bake for 6-8 minutes at 175°C/350°F, don't overbake. Best when barely brown on bottom and still soft.

Nutrition Information

- Calories: 394 calories;
- Total Fat: 22.5
- Sodium: 209
- Total Carbohydrate: 41.8
- Cholesterol: 31
- Protein: 11.8

---

170.   Twinlow Peanut Butter Cookies

Serving: 120 | Prep: 30mins | Ready in:

Ingredients

- 7 1/2 cups all-purpose flour
- 2 tablespoons baking soda
- 1 1/2 teaspoons salt
- 6 cups brown sugar
- 3 cups butter, softened
- 3 cups peanut butter
- 6 eggs
- 1/2 cup white sugar, or as needed

Direction

- Preheat an oven to 175°C/350°F.

- Line parchment paper on several baking sheets.
- Whisk salt, baking soda and flour in a bowl.
- Cream peanut butter, butter and brown sugar till smooth and evenly mixed in another big bowl.
- Beat eggs in.
- Mix flour mixture into peanut butter mixture to create smooth dough.
- Put white sugar in shallow bowl.
- Roll dough to tablespoon-sized balls; roll in white sugar till all sides are coated.
- Put cookies on prepped baking sheets, 1-in. apart minimum.
- Use fork to press each cookie flat down creating cross-cross pattern.
- In preheated oven, bake for 12 minutes till cookies are browned lightly on bottom. Cool for 5 minutes on baking sheets. Transfer to wire racks; finish cooling.

Nutrition Information

- Calories: 141 calories;
- Protein: 2.8
- Total Fat: 8.2
- Sodium: 156
- Total Carbohydrate: 15.2
- Cholesterol: 22

171.   Uncle Mac's Peanut Butter And Jelly Cookies

Serving: 12 | Prep: 20mins | Ready in:

Ingredients

- 1 cup peanut butter
- 1 cup white sugar
- 1 egg
- 1 teaspoon vanilla extract
- 2 tablespoons fruit preserves, any flavor

Direction

- Preheat oven to 175°C or 350°F.
- Whisk vanilla, egg, sugar and peanut butter in a medium-sized bowl till well blended. Drop by teaspoonfuls to the ungreased cookie sheets. Shape a crisscross pattern on the top by a fork. Form a small hole in the top of each cookie using the wooden spoon's handle. Using preserves to fill the hole.
- Bake in the preheated oven for 8 - 11 minutes. Let it cool down for several minutes on the cookie sheets prior to placing it onto wire racks to cool down totally.

Nutrition Information

- Calories: 207 calories;
- Sodium: 106
- Total Carbohydrate: 23.2
- Cholesterol: 16
- Protein: 5.9
- Total Fat: 11.3

172.   Vegan Chocolate Chip, Oatmeal, And Nut Cookies

Serving: 24 | Prep: 15mins | Ready in:

Ingredients

- 1 cup white sugar
- 1/3 cup soy milk
- 1/3 cup peanut butter
- 2 tablespoons canola oil
- 1 teaspoon pure vanilla extract
- 1 cup whole wheat flour
- 1 cup rolled oats
- 1/2 teaspoon baking soda
- 1/2 teaspoon salt
- 1/2 cup vegan semi-sweet chocolate chips
- 1/2 cup walnut pieces

Direction

- Preheat an oven to 220°C/425°F then oil big baking sheet.
- Use whisk to mix vanilla extract, canola oil, peanut butter, soymilk and sugar till fully smooth in big bowl.
- Mix salt, baking soda, oats and flour in another bowl; add to peanut butter mixture. Mix to combine; fold walnut pieces and chocolate chips into flour mixture.
- By big spoonfuls, drop batter on prepped baking sheet.
- In preheated oven, bake cookies for 10 minutes till browned along edges; cool cookies for 10 minutes on sheet. Transfer to cooling rack; fully cool.

Nutrition Information

- Calories: 112 calories;
- Total Fat: 5
- Sodium: 93
- Total Carbohydrate: 15.5
- Cholesterol: 0
- Protein: 2.5

173.   Whitney's Peanut Butter Cookie Balls

Serving: 12 | Prep: | Ready in:

Ingredients

- 1 cup peanut butter
- 1 cup butter, softened
- 2 cups confectioners' sugar
- 1 cup graham cracker crumbs
- 1 cup semisweet chocolate chips

Direction

- Combine ingredients, mix by hand, shape into balls. Dip or roll into the following ingredients: graham cracker crumbs, icing

sugar, sprinkles, cocoa, coconut. Chill and serve.

Nutrition Information

- Calories: 437 calories;
- Total Fat: 31.1
- Sodium: 252
- Total Carbohydrate: 38.3
- Cholesterol: 41
- Protein: 6.6

174.   World's Easiest Peanut Butter Blossoms

Serving: 36 | Prep: 15mins | Ready in:

Ingredients

- 1 (18 ounce) jar smooth peanut butter
- 1 1/4 cups white sugar
- 2 eggs
- 1/2 cup white sugar
- 36 milk chocolate candy kisses (such as Hershey's Kisses®), unwrapped

Direction

- Preheat an oven to 165°C/325°F.
- Mix eggs, 1 1/4 cups white sugar and peanut butter in bowl; roll to small balls.
- Put leftover 1/2 cup white sugar in bowl; roll balls in sugar till coated. Put ball on baking sheet, 1-in. apart.
- In preheated oven, bake for 12-14 minutes till edges start to crack and bottoms are very lightly browned. Press chocolate kiss immediately into middle of every cookie. Cool for 1-2 minutes on baking sheet. Put on wire racks; completely cool for 15 minutes.

Nutrition Information

- Calories: 149 calories;

- Total Fat: 8.9
- Sodium: 73
- Total Carbohydrate: 15.3
- Cholesterol: 11
- Protein: 4.2

- Total Carbohydrate: 13.2
- Cholesterol: 8
- Protein: 2.3
- Total Fat: 6.7
- Sodium: 136

175. Yummy Peanut Butter Cookies

Serving: 48 | Prep: 5mins | Ready in:

Ingredients

- 1 cup margarine
- 1 cup peanut butter
- 1 cup white sugar
- 1 cup brown sugar
- 2 eggs
- 1 teaspoon vanilla extract
- 1/2 teaspoon almond extract
- 2 1/2 cups all-purpose flour
- 1 1/2 teaspoons baking soda
- 1/2 teaspoon salt

Direction

- Preheat an oven to 190°C/375°F then grease 2 cookie sheets.
- Cream brown sugar, white sugar, peanut butter and margarine till smooth in big bowl; one by one, beat eggs in. Mix almond and vanilla extracts in. mix salt, baking soda and flour; mix into peanut butter mixture. Roll dough to 1-in. balls; put on prepped cookie sheets, 2-in. apart. Make crisscrosses on top with wet fork dipped in sugar.
- In preheated oven, bake for 8-10 minutes; cool cookies for 5 minutes on baking sheet. Transfer to wire rack; fully cool. Serve together with a glass of milk

Nutrition Information

- Calories: 120 calories;

Index

Conclusion

Thank you again for downloading this book!

I hope you enjoyed reading about my book!

If you enjoyed this book, please take the time to share your thoughts and post a review on Amazon. It'd be greatly appreciated!

Write me an honest review about the book – I truly value your opinion and thoughts and I will incorporate them into my next book, which is already underway.

Thank you!

If you have any questions, **feel free to contact at:** _author@clamrecipes.com_

Erma Ketron

clamrecipes.com

Made in the USA
Middletown, DE
14 December 2022

18570902R00051